The Anointing and The Presence

Dag Heward-Mills

Parchment House

Unless otherwise stated, all Scripture quotations are taken from the King James Version of the Bible.

Copyright © 2016 Dag Heward-Mills

THE ANOINTING AND THE PRESENCE

First published 2019 by Parchment House
1st Printing 2019

Find out more about Dag Heward-Mills at:

Healing Jesus Campaign
Email: evangelist@daghewardmills.org
Website: www.daghewardmills.org
Facebook: Dag Heward-Mills
Twitter: @EvangelistDag

ISBN: 978-1-64329-209-0

All rights reserved under international copyright law. Written permission must be secured from the publisher to use or reproduce any part of this book.

Contents

1. Why Do You Need His Presence To Go with You? 1
2. The Anointed Presence 7
3. Jehovah Shammah: God Whose Presence Can be Felt 11
4. What Defines the Presence of God? 18
5. The Presence of God is the Holy Spirit WITH US 24
6. How You Can be Anointed but Be Without the Presence of God 28
7. The Presence of God is the Glory and the Goodness of God 34
8. Who Has the Presence of God? 38
9. Serve in the Presence or out of the Presence 45
10. God's Presence in Secret Places 49
11. How You Can Enter the Presence of God With Thanksgiving 55
12. How You Can Enter the Presence of God With Praise 59
13. How to Enter the Presence of God By Being Upright 62
14. Where There is Pride The Presence of God Leaves 65
15. The Presence of God is Mysterious 76
16. The Presence of God and Prosperity 83
17. Obedience: the Master Key to The Presence of God 90
18. Benefits of the Presence of God 96
19. Divine Signs of the Presence of God in Your Ministry 104
20. Moments in the Presence of God 110

21. Strange Happenings in the Presence of God............................ 118
22. Reactions to God's Presence.. 126
23. Experience the Continuous Presence of God........................... 133
24. His Presence is a Prophecy 137

Chapter 1

Why Do You Need His Presence To Go with You?

And he said, MY PRESENCE SHALL GO WITH THEE, and I will give thee rest. And he said unto him, If thy presence go not with me, carry us not up hence.

Exodus 33:14-15

1. **You need His presence to go with you because Moses needed the presence of God to go with him.**

If Moses refused to go out into ministry without the presence of God, how can you go out into life and ministry without the presence of God? Can you compare yourself with Moses? Do you know how great Moses was? He was the greatest prophet of the Old Testament. God used him mightily. Yet, he said he would not venture out without the presence of God.

> **And he said, My presence shall go with thee, and I will give thee rest. And he said unto him, If thy presence go not with me, carry us not up hence.**
>
> **Exodus 33:14-15**

2. **You need His presence to go with you because of your weakness, your dishonour and your corruption.**

> **So also is the resurrection of the dead. It is sown in corruption; it is raised in incorruption: It is sown in dishonour; it is raised in glory: it is sown in weakness; it is raised in power: It is sown a natural body; it is raised a spiritual body. There is a natural body, and there is a spiritual body.**
>
> **1 Corinthians 15:42-44**

At your funeral, you will be put into the ground. The scripture teaches that your body will be sown in weakness, in dishonour and in corruption. The end of all men is the same. That is why we need Jesus Christ. We will all go into the ground in weakness, in dishonour and in corruption. How can someone who is weak, dishonourable and corrupt be used by God? Moses was weak, corrupt and dishonourable. He was wanted in Egypt for murder. He did not need anybody to tell him that he needed God's presence. He argued with God: "If your presence does not go with me, I am not going anywhere." I can understand him. Can't you?

3. **You need His presence to go with you because you are nothing but grass.**

   The voice said, Cry. And he said, what shall I cry? All flesh is grass, and all the goodliness thereof is as the flower of the field: The grass withereth, the flower fadeth: because the spirit of the Lord bloweth upon it: surely the people is grass. The grass withereth, the flower fadeth: but the word of our God shall stand for ever.

   Isaiah 40:6-8

   All flesh is grass! You are grass! Surely, the people is grass! You are not like grass! You are grass! Look out of your window and see the grass in the fields. Those are people. Many dead people have dissolved into the soil and have grown up as grass on the field. The grass withers! People wither! To wither is to shrivel up and dry up. All men shrivel and dry up. All men shrink out of existence. That is what it means to wither.

   The goodliness of your life is like the flower of the field. The loveliness in your life is like the flower of the field. All flowers fade! Indeed, they fade very quickly. All men fade! Indeed, they fade very quickly. All men gradually lose their brightness, their freshness and their colour.

   What can grass accomplish? What can withering grass accomplish? What can a fading flower accomplish? Nothing! You are nothing but withering grass and a fading flower! Without the presence of God, you can do and will do nothing. We need the presence of God to do anything.

4. **You need His presence to go with you because you are a man of unclean lips.**

   Then said I, Woe is me! For I am undone; because I am a man of unclean lips, and I dwell in the midst of a people of unclean lips: for mine eyes have seen the King, the Lord of hosts.

   Isaiah 6:5

A man of unclean lips cannot accomplish very much. Remember that you will be preaching out of these very lips. Your sin, your uncleanness and your wickedness are not things we are making up. They are real. Isaiah was shocked to find how unclean he was. Without the presence of God, a man of unclean lips is going nowhere.

5. **You need His presence to go with you because without Him you can do nothing.**

I am the vine, ye are the branches: He that abideth in me, and I in him, the same bringeth forth much fruit: for without me ye can do nothing.

John 15:5

Jesus was clear; without Him, you can do nothing! He did not say you can do a few things. He did not say you can do some minor things. He did not say you can do a few spiritual things. He said, "You can do nothing!" Nothing means zero! Nothing means nothing! But with God, all things are possible! Once God is present in your life, your nothingness is converted into something.

You need him because you need to be endued with power to be able to do anything for God.

And, behold, I send the promise of my Father upon you: but tarry ye in the city of Jerusalem, until ye be ENDUED WITH POWER from on high.

Luke 24:49

Until you are endued with power, you can do nothing. In the presence of God, you will be endued with power. Jesus warned His corrupt, proud and weak disciples to stay in the city until they were endued with power.

6. **You need His presence to go with you because it will transform your destiny.**

And he lighted upon a certain place, and tarried there all night, because the sun was set; and he took of the stones of that place, and put them for his pillows, and lay down in that place to sleep. And he dreamed, and behold a ladder set up on the earth, and the top of it reached to heaven: and behold the angels of God ascending and descending on it. And, behold, the Lord stood above it, and said, I am the Lord God of Abraham thy father, and the God of Isaac: the land whereon thou liest, to thee will I give it, and to thy seed; And thy seed shall be as the dust of the earth, and thou shalt spread abroad to the west, and to the east, and to the north, and to the south: and in thee and in thy seed shall all the families of the earth be blessed. And, BEHOLD, I AM WITH THEE, AND WILL KEEP THEE IN ALL PLACES WHITHER THOU GOEST, and will bring thee again into this land; for I will not leave thee, until I have done that which I have spoken to thee of.

Genesis 28:11-15

Jacob turned into the great Israel we know by having the presence of God with him. God appeared to Jacob and promised him His presence. It was His presence that guided Jacob through all his journeys. It was the presence of God that gave Jacob the many children that he had. It was the presence of God that made Jacob give birth to so many sons. It was the presence of God that made Jacob prosper. It was the presence of God that made Jacob overcome the cheating and swindling by Laban. It was the presence of God that made Jacob overcome the family problems he had from his children. It was the presence of God that enabled Jacob to see Joseph again. It was the presence of God that made Jacob live long enough to see his grandchildren. It was the presence of God that turned the descendants of Jacob into the greatest and most unique nation on earth.

7. You need His presence to go with you because the Lord thy God in the midst of thee is mighty.

The Lord thy God in the midst of thee is mighty; he will save, he will rejoice over thee with joy; he will rest in his love, he will joy over thee with singing.
Zephaniah 3:17

When God is in the midst of you, you are greatly blessed. He will save you! He will help you! He will deliver you! He will rejoice over you! He will rejoice over you with singing!

Chapter 2

The Anointed Presence

Whither shall I go from THY SPIRIT? or whither shall I flee from THY PRESENCE?

Psalms 139:7

This book is all about "the anointed presence". This book is not about the presence of an ordinary human being nor is it about the presence of any important personality you know. What is the anointed presence? It is the presence of someone more special than any human being can ever be. Whenever this anointed presence is there, people experience many good things. Today, many ministries do not have an anointed presence.

What exactly is an anointed presence? There are different dimensions of this mystical presence. The anointed presence is the holy presence of God in your life. The anointed presence is the presence of the Holy Spirit. The anointed presence is the holy presence of Jesus Christ in your life. The anointed presence is the presence of our Lord in your life. The anointed presence is the holy presence of His glory in your life. The anointed presence is the presence of the holy angels.

It is the holy presence of God that makes a big difference to everything. It is the presence of the Holy Spirit that makes a big difference. As you read this book, I pray that you will stop yearning for the presence of human beings and desire to have the anointed presence of God in your life. Stop yearning for the presence of presidents, vice presidents and other politicians. Stop looking to human beings! Stop desiring mere human personalities! Stop desiring that certain people would be at your programme. What will make the difference is the anointed presence of God.

Start yearning for the presence of the greatest person of all! The anointed holy presence is important for your life and ministry.

1. The presence of God

> For Christ is not entered into the holy places made with hands, which are the figures of the true; but into heaven itself, now to appear in THE PRESENCE OF GOD for us:
>
> Hebrews 9:24

2. The presence of the Holy Spirit

Cast me not away from thy presence; and take not thy holy spirit from me.

Psalms 51:11

3. The presence of Jesus Christ

For what is our hope, or joy, or crown of rejoicing? Are not even ye in the PRESENCE OF OUR LORD JESUS CHRIST at his coming?

1 Thessalonians 2:19

4. The presence of the Lord

Who shall be punished with everlasting destruction from the PRESENCE OF THE LORD, and from the glory of his power;

2 Thessalonians 1:9

5. The presence of His glory

Now unto him that is able to keep you from falling, and to present you faultless before the PRESENCE OF HIS GLORY with exceeding joy,

Jude 1:24

6. The presence of the Lamb

The same shall drink of the wine of the wrath of God, which is poured out without mixture into the cup of his indignation; and he shall be tormented with fire and brimstone in the presence of the holy angels, and IN THE PRESENCE OF THE LAMB:

Revelation 14:10

7. The presence of the Holy Angels

Wherever the presence of God is you always have angels.

The same shall drink of the wine of the wrath of God, which is poured out without mixture into the cup of his indignation; and he shall be tormented with fire and brimstone IN THE PRESENCE OF THE HOLY ANGELS, and in the presence of the Lamb:

Revelation 14:10

Chapter 3

Jehovah Shammah: God Whose Presence Can be Felt

> It was round about eighteen thousand measures: and the name of the city from that day shall be, THE LORD IS THERE (JEHOVAH SHAMMAH).
>
> Ezekiel 48:35

1. Follow the presence of God and get to know God whose presence can be felt.

Jehovah Shammah is the God whose presence can be felt. Jehovah Shammah means, "The Lord is there!" "The Lord is present!" It is possible to grow in the faith and experience the presence of God in a real way. You can become someone who knows when God is there.

There are many ways in which you can know God. You can get to know God as your healer (Jehovah Rophe). You can also get to know God as your financier, your provider (Jehovah Jireh) or even your shepherd (Jehovah Ra-ah). Indeed, you can also get to know God as someone who is present and whose presence can be felt (Jehovah Shammah).

There are ministers who know God as Jehovah Jireh. They are sure that He is a provider and they are able to relate with God as someone who gives them money and provisions. Some pastors do not know how to relate with God as Jehovah Jireh. They know Him as a conservative and moral God. But they do not know the aspect of God that has to do with provision. There are other ministers who know God as a healer but do not know Him as a financial provider. Indeed, we all know different aspects of God to different extents.

In this book, I am sharing that you can know God in yet another way. You can know Jehovah Shammah, the Lord who is present in a real way. You can know the aura of God's presence. You can feel His presence and you can be impressed with His presence. Few people enjoy His presence as they should! God is real! It is possible to grow in your ability to experience God. You can experience His presence in your room! You can experience His presence in your meetings! You can experience His presence at home. You can feel His presence in a real way. That is Jehovah Shammah!

And it came to pass on a certain day, as he was teaching, that there were Pharisees and doctors of the law sitting by, which were come out of every town of Galilee, and

Judaea, and Jerusalem: and **THE POWER OF THE LORD WAS PRESENT TO HEAL THEM.**

Luke 5:17

Jesus could sense the presence of God. He knew when the power of God was present. Jesus knew when the power of God was present. That is why His healing ministry was so successful. It is not always that the power of God is present. You can become someone who knows the Lord's presence. You will know when He is in the room and when He is not. You will know when He is standing in front of you. You will be impressed with the sensation of His awesome, dignified presence. You will know when God is there and when God will work wonders. You will also know when He is not there.

2. Follow the presence of God and experience divine growth.

I WILL BE AS THE DEW UNTO ISRAEL: he shall GROW as the lily, and cast forth his ROOTS as Lebanon. His BRANCHES shall spread, and his BEAUTY shall be as the olive tree, and his SMELL as Lebanon.

Hosea 14:5-6

God will come to you as the dew. Dew is invisible. Dew is invisible rain! The prophetic effects of this invisible rain is the watering of your life. The presence of God cannot be seen. However, you can see the effects of His presence. This is why the presence of God is likened to dew. God says He will be like the dew to Israel. He will be the invisible growth factor to Israel.

The invisible presence of God has fantastic effects on your life. The effect of His presence is GROWTH! You will grow as a lily.

The effect of His presence is ROOTS! You will have deep roots as in Lebanon. The effect of His presence is BRANCHES! Your branches will spread far and wide. The effect of His presence is BEAUTY! Your life will be even more and more beautiful. The effect of His presence is a GOOD SMELL! You will smell like Lebanon and will be detected and noticed from afar.

3. Follow the presence of God and win all your battles.

And they commanded the people, saying, when ye see the ark of the covenant of the Lord your God, and the priests the Levites bearing it, then ye shall remove from your place, and GO AFTER IT.

Joshua 3:3

Following the presence of God was the master key given to Joshua the General. Victory was guaranteed when the Israelites followed the presence of God.

In the New Testament, we have an instruction similar to the one given to Joshua. Joshua was asked to follow the ark! We have been asked to go after spiritual gifts!

Even so ye, forasmuch as ye are zealous of spiritual gifts, seek that ye may excel to the edifying of the church.

1 Corinthians 14:12

"Go after spiritual gifts. Covet earnestly the best gifts!" But covet earnestly the best gifts: and yet shew I unto you a more excellent way"(1 Corinthians 12:31).

The more you seek after spiritual gifts as a minister, the more you will experience growth. Seek to super-abound in spiritual gifts. Desire the best gifts! Desire the highest kind of ministry! Desire the presence of God in everything you do! You must follow the presence of God until you overcome in all your battles.

4. Follow the presence of God and you will go deeper.

As you follow the presence of God, you will come to His perfect will for your life. Everyone who entered the ministry experienced the presence of God in a special way. When Abraham,

Jacob, Moses and the disciples experienced the presence of God, they became famous ministers whose names can never be forgotten on this earth. Just a little contact with God's presence will change your life forever.

Notice how all these people went deeper when they experienced the presence of God. They no longer remained ordinary Christians but dived deep into the ministry and the service of the Lord.

a. Abraham experienced the presence of God when he was called.

AND WHEN ABRAM WAS NINETY YEARS OLD AND NINE, THE LORD APPEARED TO ABRAM, and said unto him, I am the Almighty God; walk before me, and be thou perfect. And I will make my covenant between me and thee, and will multiply thee exceedingly. And Abram fell on his face: and God talked with him, saying, As for me, behold, my covenant is with thee, and thou shalt be a father of many nations.

Genesis 17:1-4

b. Jacob experienced the presence of God when he was called.

AND JACOB WAS LEFT ALONE; AND THERE WRESTLED A MAN WITH HIM UNTIL THE BREAKING OF THE DAY. And when he saw that he prevailed not against him, he touched the hollow of his thigh; and the hollow of Jacob's thigh was out of joint, as he wrestled with him. And he said, Let me go, for the day breaketh. And he said, I will not let thee go, except thou bless me. And he said unto him, what is thy name? And he said, Jacob. And he said, Thy name shall be called no more Jacob, but Israel: for as a prince hast thou power with God and with men, and hast prevailed.

Genesis 32:24-28

c. Moses experienced the presence of God when he was called.

Now Moses kept the flock of Jethro his father in law, the priest of Midian: and he led the flock to the backside of the desert, and came to the mountain of God, even to Horeb. AND THE ANGEL OF THE LORD APPEARED UNTO HIM IN A FLAME OF FIRE OUT OF THE MIDST OF A BUSH: and he looked, and, behold, the bush burned with fire, and the bush was not consumed.

Exodus 3:1-2

d. Ezekiel experienced the presence of God when he was called.

Now it came to pass in the thirtieth year, in the fourth month, in the fifth day of the month, AS I WAS AMONG THE CAPTIVES BY THE RIVER OF CHEBAR, THAT THE HEAVENS WERE OPENED, AND I SAW VISIONS OF GOD. In the fifth day of the month, which was the fifth year of king Jehoiachin's captivity, the word of the Lord came expressly unto Ezekiel the priest, the son of Buzi, in the land of the Chaldeans by the river Chebar; and the hand of the Lord was there upon him.

And I looked, and, behold, a whirlwind came out of the north, a great cloud, and a fire infolding itself, and a brightness was about it, and out of the midst thereof as the colour of amber, out of the midst of the fire.

Ezekiel 1:1-4

e. Jesus' ministry began with the presence of God.

And THE HOLY GHOST DESCENDED IN A BODILY SHAPE LIKE A DOVE UPON HIM, AND A VOICE CAME FROM HEAVEN, WHICH SAID, THOU ART MY BELOVED SON; in thee I am well pleased. And Jesus himself began to be about thirty years of age, being (as was supposed) the son of Joseph, which was the son of Heli,

Luke 3:22-23

f. The disciples began their ministry when the presence of God came upon them.

And when the day of Pentecost was fully come, they were all with one accord in one place. And suddenly there came a sound from heaven as of a rushing mighty wind, and it filled all the house where they were sitting. And there appeared unto them cloven tongues like as of fire, and it sat upon each of them. And they were all filled with the Holy Ghost, and began to speak with other tongues, as the Spirit gave them utterance.

Acts 2:1-4

5. Follow the presence of God and you will have light and guidance for every stage of your life.

And the Lord went before them by day in a pillar of a cloud, to lead them the way; and by night in a pillar of fire, to give them light; to go by day and night:

Exodus 13:21

Follow the presence of God! Move as the presence of God moves! Move away from ministries that do not have the presence of God. Notice what it is like when preachers no longer have the presence of God with them. Go where the presence of God is. The presence of God makes all the difference! If God's presence is not in a huge cathedral do not waste your time going there. If God's presence is found in a classroom you must go there. Avoid churches and ministers that no longer have the presence of God. When you follow the pillar of fire, you will have light, revelation, illumination and direction for your life.

Chapter 4

What Defines the Presence of God?

> **And they heard the voice of the Lord God walking in the garden in the cool of the day: and Adam and his wife hid themselves from the presence of the Lord God amongst the trees of the garden.**
>
> **Genesis 3:8**

The presence of God has three elements to it: the aura of God, the voice of God and the gift of God.

1. The aura of a person reveals his presence; the aura of God reveals His presence:

And he shewed me a pure river of water of life, clear as crystal, proceeding out of THE THRONE OF GOD AND OF THE LAMB. In the midst of the street of it, and on either side of the river, was there the tree of life, which bare twelve manner of fruits, and yielded her fruit every month: and the leaves of the tree were for the healing of the nations. And there shall be no more curse: but the throne of God and of the Lamb shall be in it; and his servants shall serve him: AND THEY SHALL SEE HIS FACE; AND HIS NAME SHALL BE IN THEIR FOREHEADS. AND THERE SHALL BE NO NIGHT THERE; AND THEY NEED NO CANDLE, NEITHER LIGHT OF THE SUN; FOR THE LORD GOD GIVETH THEM LIGHT: AND THEY SHALL REIGN FOR EVER AND EVER.

Revelation 22:1-5

The aura of a person is the first evidence of a person's presence. The aura of a person speaks of the sensation and the impression that you experience when a person is present. The aura of God's presence transforms the new heaven and the new earth. The aura of His presence removes the need for the sun. They actually see His face and His throne. There is a real impression that God is present in the new heaven and the new earth.

When your father is in the house, there is a sensation and an impression of his existence. He may not talk to you and he may not call for you but there is a knowing that he is present in the house. It is this aura of a person's existence that disappears when a person dies. That is the aura of a person. When people no longer walk with God, they lose this aura. You may have the gift of God working in your life but you may not have this aura in your life.

2. The voice of a person shows his presence; the voice of God shows His presence:

> And the eyes of them both were opened, and they knew that they were naked; and they sewed fig leaves together, and made themselves aprons. And they heard the voice of the Lord God walking in the garden in the cool of the day: and Adam and his wife HID THEMSELVES FROM THE PRESENCE OF THE LORD GOD amongst the trees of the garden. And the Lord God called unto Adam, and said unto him, Where art thou? AND HE SAID, I HEARD THY VOICE IN THE GARDEN, and I was afraid, because I was naked; and I hid myself.
>
> Genesis 3:7-10

The voice of a person is the second important evidence of his presence.

The voice of God was heard in the garden because the presence of God was there. The voice of a person is clear evidence that the person is present. When Adam and Eve were driven out of the Garden of Eden, they would no longer hear God's voice in the cool of the day. They still had the whole earth before them. They still had some kind of dominion over the earth. They still had the gift of life but God's presence was no longer with them. They would no longer sense His presence in the cool of the day and they would no longer hear His voice.

When God is with you, you will hear His voice. Hearing His voice must be your great desire because it is the sign of His presence in your life. When you hear His voice speaking to you in the morning, it is a sign of His presence with you. When you hear His voice speaking to you in church, it is a sign of His presence in the church.

When your father is at home, you will hear his voice. He may call for someone. He may shout your name. He may send you to do something. He may give his advice, whether it is wanted or not. He may talk endlessly about things that you do not think are important. But that is the evidence of his presence and his existence! You may have the gift of God working in your life. You may be able to preach and teach but it may have been a long time since you heard His voice speaking to you.

3. **The gifts of a person shows his presence; the gifts of God shows His presence:**

> And I heard a great voice out of heaven saying, Behold, the tabernacle of God is with men, and he will dwell with them, and they shall be his people, and God himself shall be with them, and be their God. AND GOD SHALL WIPE AWAY ALL TEARS FROM THEIR EYES; AND THERE SHALL BE NO MORE DEATH, NEITHER SORROW, NOR CRYING, NEITHER SHALL THERE BE ANY MORE PAIN: FOR THE FORMER THINGS ARE PASSED AWAY.
>
> And he that sat upon the throne said, Behold, I make all things new. And he said unto me, write: for these words are true and faithful.
>
> Revelation 21:3-5

The presence of God in the new heaven and earth comes along with the gifts and the good things that God has. All needs are wiped away. The curse of poverty, lack, disease, death and every other thing that has plagued our lives is removed by the presence of God. Indeed, the presence of God comes with His goodness, His gifts and His nice things.

The gifts, possessions and properties of a person are the third evidence of his existence. When your father is at home, he will give you his money, his gifts and his nice things. This is the part of the presence of God that we enjoy the most; His gifts and His goodness. However, this is the part of the presence of God that can deceive you. Gifts and good things, once given, are not withdrawn. The gifts and callings of God are without repentance. When God withdraws His voice and His being from you, you may be deceived by the presence of His gifts and His nice things.

For the gifts and calling of God are without repentance.

Romans 11:29

Your father may give you a house but he himself may not be in the house.

He may give you some money and you may walk away with that and still walk away from His presence. In the same way, many people may have the anointing and the gifts of God but are far from His presence. This is why I say that if I had to choose between the anointing and the presence of God, I would choose the presence of God. The presence of God has all three elements: the aura, the voice and the gifts!

I once knew a young man to whom I gave an expensive wedding present. After some years, he became a painfully rebellious person. Even though this young man had turned into a disloyal and hateful rebel, I did not go back for the present I had bought for him.

I was no longer a part of his life. I no longer advised him as I used to. I never said a word about anything that he did or did not do. I never went to his house or his church and I was no longer present in the major events of his life, even though he wanted me to be. This man had my gift but he no longer had my real presence.

The presence of God is made up of these three elements: the aura of His presence, the voice of His presence and the gifts of His presence.

So, if you had to choose between the presence of God and the anointing, which one would you ask for?

You are more likely to ask for the anointing instead of the presence of God because you do not know what the presence of God is.

Why would you choose the anointing of God when you could have the presence of God? The presence of God is the anointing of God plus more!

The anointing of the Holy Spirit is the empowerment to work for God. Jesus said, "The Spirit of the Lord is upon me because He has anointed me to preach, to heal and to set the captives free." (Luke 4:18). The anointing on your life empowers you to do spiritual works like preaching, teaching, healing and setting captives free. The anointing of God is what we call the gifts of the Spirit and the gifts of ministry. The gifts of prophecy, the gift of healing, the gifts of word of knowledge and wisdom are given to make you minister, to make you preach and to make you heal.

The presence of God is even better. Think about it! The presence of a person is far greater than the presence of his gift. The presence of God has three elements whereas the anointing of God has only one. There are many ministers who have received the gift of God but have walked on without the presence of God.

Indeed, only a spiritual person can detect that the presence of God is not in a church. The gifts and calling of God are without repentance. Many churches and ministries that seem to be in full bloom actually lack the presence of God. The presence of God has long departed from there.

Chapter 5

The Presence of God is the Holy Spirit WITH US

THE LORD THY GOD IN THE MIDST OF THEE IS MIGHTY; he will save, he will rejoice over thee with joy; he will rest in his love, he will joy over thee with singing.

Zephaniah 3:17

The Holy Spirit maintains three important relationships with believers:
1. The Holy Spirit upon us.
2. The Holy Spirit in us.
3. The Holy Spirit with us.

All these three relationships are so relevant and so important for us. There are some important definitions that must be clarified before we continue this study. What we normally call the anointing is the Holy Spirit upon us.

What we call the presence of God is what we normally call the Holy Spirit with us.

What we call the Holy Spirit baptism is actually the Spirit in us.

Each of these relationships of the Holy Spirit with us is unique and produces special and wonderful results in our lives.

The Holy Spirit Upon Us

1. The Holy Spirit upon us is what we call the anointing.
We call the Holy Spirit upon us the anointing because of what Jesus said in Luke 4:18

THE SPIRIT OF THE LORD IS UPON ME, BECAUSE HE HATH ANOINTED ME to preach the gospel to the poor; he hath sent me to heal the brokenhearted, to preach deliverance to the captives, and recovering of sight to the blind, to set at liberty them that are bruised, to preach the acceptable year of the Lord.

Luke 4:18-19

Jesus said He was anointed because the Spirit of the Lord was upon Him. When the Spirit of the Lord is upon you, you are anointed. When you are anointed, as Jesus described, you are empowered to work for God. Luke 4:18,19 describes how Jesus was empowered to preach the gospel to the poor, empowered to heal the broken hearted, empowered to open blind eyes, empowered to set captives free and empowered to preach the acceptable year of the Lord. Based on this scripture, the anointing is the empowerment to work for God and to do the things you have to do in ministry.

In the Old Testament, only the prophets, the king and priests were anointed and empowered to work for God. However, in the New Testament, more people are anointed and given gifts that enable them to work. Pastors, evangelists, prophets, singers and helpers are all given the gifts of the Holy Spirit, which are the anointing of the Holy Spirit.

The Holy Spirit in Us

2. **The Holy Spirit in us is what we call the Holy Spirit baptism.** We say this because when Jesus promised that we would be baptized with the Holy Spirit, He said that the Holy Spirit was already with us but would then be in us.

And I will pray the Father, and he shall give you another Comforter, that he may abide with you for ever; even THE SPIRIT of truth; whom the world cannot receive, because it seeth him not, neither knoweth him: but ye know him; for he dwelleth with you, and SHALL BE IN YOU.

John 14:16-17

The Holy Spirit in us causes us to speak in tongues and to become witnesses of Jesus Christ. Where the influence of the Holy Spirit in us is not strong, people do not speak in tongues and do not evangelize.

The Holy Spirit with Us

3. **The Holy Spirit with us is what we call the presence of God. God with us!** That God would be with us wherever

we go and in whatever we do is what we call the presence of God.

Even the Spirit of truth; whom the world cannot receive, because it seeth him not, neither knoweth him: but ye know him; for he dwelleth with you, and shall be in you.

John 14:17

This is the oldest relationship that the Holy Spirit has had with human beings. All through the Old Testament, it was the presence of the Holy Spirit that gave victory to the Israelites.

THE LORD THY GOD IN THE MIDST OF THEE IS MIGHTY; he will save, he will rejoice over thee with joy; he will rest in his love, he will joy over thee with singing.

Zephaniah 3:17

In the New Testament, Jesus promised a richer relationship with the Holy Spirit. That was the Holy Spirit in us. He also promised that more people would have the Holy Spirit.

Chapter 6

How You Can be Anointed but be Without the Presence of God

And she said, The Philistines be upon thee, Samson. And he awoke out of his sleep, and said, I will go out as at other times before, and shake myself. And he wist not that THE LORD WAS DEPARTED from him.

Judges 16:20

When the Bible speaks about the Holy Spirit, it often does not clarify whether it is the Spirit upon you, the Spirit with you or the Spirit in you. You have to deduce from the context whether the presence of the Holy Spirit is the Spirit upon you, the Spirit in you or the Spirit with you.

The Spirit upon you is the gift of God. The scripture says that the gifts and calling of God are without repentance. Therefore God does not take away His gifts from a person.

> **For the gifts and calling of God are without repentance.**
> **Romans 11:29**

Since the presence of God is the person of God, you may continue to have the gift but He Himself, the Giver of the gift may not be with you. I can give you a gift but I may not be with you as you enjoy the gift. I can give you my car as a gift but not be with you as you drive the car. On the other hand, I can give you a Bible as a gift and live with you as well. That is marriage! In my life, I have given many people Bibles as gifts. However, it is only to my wife that I have given the gift of a Bible as well as the gift of my presence.

A number of people illustrate this mysterious principle of having the anointing but losing the presence of God.

1. Saul

> **Then Samuel took the horn of oil, and anointed him in the midst of his brethren: and the Spirit of the Lord came upon David from that day forward. So Samuel rose up, and went to Ramah. But THE SPIRIT OF THE LORD DEPARTED FROM SAUL, and an evil spirit from the Lord troubled him.**
> **1 Samuel 16:13-14**

This explains the story of Saul who was anointed to be the king and remained anointed as the king to the end of his life. God never took away the anointing of kingship from him. David came near but was afraid to touch Saul, because Saul was anointed. The reason David did not want to kill Saul was because Saul was anointed. However, we read in the Bible that the Spirit of God left Saul. So Saul operated the anointing of kingship to the end of his life but without the presence of the Spirit in a certain way. Saul maintained the gift of kingship to the very end but Saul also lost the presence of the Spirit!

2. **David**

Cast me not away from thy presence; and TAKE NOT THY HOLY SPIRIT FROM ME.

Psalms 51:11

King David knew that he could also lose the presence of the Spirit. He had seen what happened to Saul. He knew the presence of God could leave him even though he was still the king. He knew what happened to Saul so he cried, "Do not take away your presence from me." King David knew that he could be the king alright, but the presence of God would not be with him. He could have the gift of the throne but would be without the presence of God. He would continue to minister as a psalmist but the presence of God would not be with him.

3. **Samson**

And she said, The Philistines be upon thee, Samson. And he awoke out of his sleep, and said, I will go out as at other times before, and shake myself. And he wist not that THE LORD WAS DEPARTED from him.

Judges 16:20

When Samson revealed his secret to Delilah, he put himself in great danger. The presence of God left him. This led to a change in his ministry. He suffered setbacks and his circumstances changed completely. However, true to the word of God, the gifts and callings of God never changed and he was empowered to fight on and do the work of God even in that modified and weakened situation.

And Samson called unto the Lord, and said, O Lord God, remember me, I pray thee, and strengthen me, I pray thee, only this once, O God, that I may be at once avenged of the Philistines for my two eyes.

And Samson took hold of the two middle pillars upon which the house stood, and on which it was borne up, of the one with his right hand, and of the other with his left.

And Samson said, let me die with the Philistines. And he bowed himself with all his might; and the house fell upon the lords, and upon all the people that were therein. So the dead which he slew at his death were more than they which he slew in his life.

Judges 16:28-30

Today there are many ministers who are in difficulty and are in a "modified" situation. Sometimes, they look awkward in their new circumstances where the presence of God has departed from them. They continue to minister from their weakened, modified situation and are often a far cry from when the presence of God was in full manifestation in their lives.

Samson experienced this. Temporarily, he was unable to fight the Philistines because the Spirit departed from him. But even in his blind fallen state, the power of God came back to him and he was able to fight the Philistines. In a sense the power to work for God never left him till he died. The departure of the presence of God is what changed his ministry. He simply continued to operate in ministry from a weakened state.

4. Judas

And after the sop Satan entered into him. Then said Jesus unto him, That thou doest, do quickly.

John 13:27

Judas is another person who received the gift of God and became anointed to work for God. He was one of the twelve disciples sent out to heal, teach and freely minister the power of

God. Jesus Himself did not strike out Judas because he was one of His anointed apostles and disciples. He warned him several times but Judas took no heed. Judas walked away from the presence of the Holy Spirit. Judas was destroyed when he went away from the presence of Jesus.

But, behold, the hand of him that betrayeth me is with me on the table. And truly the Son of man goeth, as it was determined: but woe unto that man by whom he is betrayed!

Luke 22:21-22

The presence of God is the goodness of God, and the presence of His person with you. Having a gift and being able to work for God is not the same as having the presence of God with you.

In the parable of the wheat and tares, Jesus revealed a startling truth. He said that the tares and the wheat (those with the presence of God and those without the presence of God) were remarkably similar. If you ever see a picture of wheat and tares you will understand why Jesus warned not to touch the wheat. They are so similar that you will destroy a large portion of wheat in your bid to root out the tares.

He said unto them, An enemy hath done this. The servants said unto him, Wilt thou then that we go and gather them up? But he said, Nay; lest while ye gather up the tares, ye root up also the wheat with them.

Matthew 13:28-29

Those who carry the presence of God and those who do not, are very similar in their appearance. It is often not easy to tell that the presence of God has departed from a minister. Perhaps the only way you may be able to see this difference is in the fruit. Tares or weeds do not bear fruit. Weeds do not bear fruit!

The sign of the Holy Spirit's presence in the early church was the winning of souls and bearing witness of Jesus Christ.

Today, the reaping in of dollars, pounds and euros, rather than the reaping of souls, are used as markers of success. We do not need markers of success. We need markers of the presence of the Holy Spirit!

Chapter 7

The Presence of God is the Glory and the Goodness of God

And he said, My presence shall go with thee, and I will give thee rest. And he said unto him, IF THY PRESENCE GO NOT WITH ME, CARRY US NOT UP HENCE. For wherein shall it be known here that I and thy people have found grace in thy sight? IS IT NOT IN THAT THOU GOEST WITH US? so shall we be separated, I and thy people, from all the people that are upon the face of the earth. And the Lord said unto Moses, I WILL DO THIS THING also that thou hast spoken: for thou hast found grace in my sight, and I know thee by name. And he said, I beseech thee, SHEW ME THY GLORY.

Exodus 33:14-18

From the scripture above, we see Moses negotiating with God for His presence to go with them. The Lord agreed to answer Moses' prayer. *I will go with you. I will show you my presence and I will show you my glory.* The presence of God is the glory and the goodness of God. God's answer to Moses' request for His presence was to show His glory, His goodness, His mercies, His graciousness and His name.

1. The presence of the Holy Spirit is the glory of God.

   And he said, I beseech thee, shew me thy glory.

   Exodus 33:18

2. The presence of the Holy Spirit is the goodness of God.

   And he said, I will make all my GOODNESS pass before thee, and I will proclaim the name of the Lord before thee; and will be gracious to whom I will be gracious, and will shew mercy on whom I will shew mercy.

   Exodus 33:19

3. The presence of the Holy Spirit is the name of God.

   And he said, I will make all my goodness pass before thee, and I will proclaim THE NAME OF THE LORD before thee; and will be gracious to whom I will be gracious, and will shew mercy on whom I will shew mercy.

   Exodus 33:19

4. The presence of the Holy Spirit is the graciousness of God.

   And he said, I will make all my goodness pass before thee, and I will proclaim the name of the Lord before thee; and WILL BE GRACIOUS to whom I will be gracious, and will shew mercy on whom I will shew mercy.

   Exodus 33:19

5. The presence of the Holy Spirit is the mercy of God.

And he said, I will make all my goodness pass before thee, and I will proclaim the name of the Lord before thee; and will be gracious to whom I will be gracious, and will shew MERCY on whom I will shew mercy.

Exodus 33:19

All these definitions of the presence of the Lord are revealed from the revelation Moses had when he asked to see the presence of God. When the Lord eventually showed him His presence and passed before him, great declarations were made. These great declarations revealed the goodness, the kindness, the graciousness and the merciful loving character of God.

The presence of God, therefore, reveals the good, loving and wonderful nature of God. This is the same thing we experience when we get close to people and experience their presence. We get to know their true character and nature. When you live in someone's presence, you will find out if they are lazy, if they are wicked or if they are loving.

I once had a close interaction with a man who was a pastor of a church. After my close interaction with this individual, I came away with the feeling of having met an extortionist, a malicious person and a Lucifer. In spite of his soft-spoken presentation, I came away from this person's presence with a very negative impression.

Getting up close and personal with anyone will most likely reveal the person's true nature.

Marriage is another encounter with a person's presence that reveals their true nature. *Marriage is where you live in the presence of an individual almost continually. It is there that you discover the qualities, good or bad that a person has.* You discover if the person is loving, kind, patient or otherwise.

Indeed, you may discover a person who is lazy, wicked, incompetent and downright evil. In marriage, you discover a person's fears, anxieties, complexes and way of thinking. Being in the presence of a person reveals all these things.

This is exactly what happened to Moses. He experienced the presence of God and thereby experienced His goodness, His mercy and His graciousness.

I once heard many bad stories about a certain pastor. One day I had an opportunity to interact with him. Although this person shouted and behaved badly, I came away with an impression of having dealt with a person who was essentially good but perhaps uneducated. In the presence of a person, you truly encounter his nature.

Chapter 8

Who Has the Presence of God?

> Now when they saw the boldness of Peter and John, and perceived that they were unlearned and ignorant men, they marvelled; and they took knowledge of them, that **THEY HAD BEEN WITH JESUS.**
>
> Acts 4:13

1. Those who preach about Jesus and salvation have the presence of God with them.

Neither is there SALVATION in any other: for there is none other name under heaven given among men, whereby WE MUST BE SAVED.

Now when they saw the boldness of Peter and John, and perceived that they were unlearned and ignorant men, they marvelled; and they took knowledge of them, THAT THEY HAD BEEN WITH JESUS. And beholding the man which was healed standing with them, they could say nothing against it.

Acts 4:12-14

Ministers who have the presence of God usually preach about salvation. *Ministers who have the presence of God preach about Jesus Christ and not about economics, money, empowerment or the market place.* Watching Christian television or interacting with men of God will quickly lead you to the conclusion that "not all men of God have the presence of God with them".

How can that be? Indeed all men of God quote scripture. All men of God claim to represent God. All the men of God seem to declare wonderful things about a great God. Yet many do not have the presence of God with them. With experience you will be able to detect this by a simple conversation with a man of God. Listening or watching a man of God for just a minute is enough to know whether the presence of God is present or not.

Who are those who have the presence of God?

Those who have the presence of God are easy to pick out. Even the wicked Pharisees were able to detect the presence of God in the disciples of Christ. They noticed the mention of Jesus Christ in the words of these young men. They noticed that these men were talking and preaching about Jesus Christ.

Today people preach about success, self-achievement, prosperity and economics. These simple disciples were speaking about Jesus Christ and pure salvation. The Pharisees noticed the unmistakable miracle that had been performed. They could detect the presence of God in these men of God. Where are your miracles? What are your preaching topics? Your preaching topics and the power of God will tell everyone about whether the presence of God is there or not.

2. Those who stay in fellowship for long times have the presence of God.

> Wherefore of these MEN WHICH HAVE COMPANIED WITH us all the time that the Lord Jesus went in and out among us, Beginning from the baptism of John, unto that same day that he was taken up from us, must one be ordained to be a witness with us of his resurrection.
>
> Acts 1:21-22

The disciples needed to choose someone who had fellowshipped with Jesus for a long time.

Those who stay in church for long hours have the presence of God. Those who company with God are those we really need to hear from. Those who have really experienced God are those who carry the true words of God. We don't need human ideas. We need the reality of God. That is why a person who had companied with Jesus for three years was chosen to replace the missing apostle. We don't need high-sounding phrases nor do we need motivational speeches for our lives. We need to hear from God. We need something from God's presence.

It is time to be one of the men of God who has the presence of God around him. Who are those who really have the presence of God? Who are those precious men of God that we really need to listen to?

3. Those who praise God and worship Him have the presence of God.

Enter into his gates with thanksgiving, and into his courts with praise: be thankful unto him, and bless his name.

Psalms 100:4

Starting a service with praises and worship is a well-known key to entering into an atmosphere of the presence of God.

4. Those who have a thankful spirit have the presence of God.

Enter into his gates with thanksgiving, and into his courts with praise: be thankful unto him, and bless his name.

Psalms 100:4

And be not drunk with wine, wherein is excess; but be filled with the Spirit; Speaking to yourselves in psalms and hymns and spiritual songs, singing and making melody in your heart to the Lord; Giving thanks always for all things unto God and the Father in the name of our Lord Jesus Christ; Submitting yourselves one to another in the fear of God.

Ephesians 5:18-21

One of the fastest ways to lose the presence of God is to criticize and to complain. The opposite of praise is criticism. You can lose the presence of God by being critical, murmuring and speaking evil. On the other hand a grateful spirit and a thankful heart is key to experiencing the presence of God.

5. Those who are prayerful have the presence of God.

And when they had prayed, the place was shaken where they were assembled together; and they were all filled with the Holy Ghost, and they spake the word of God with boldness.

Acts 4:31

Those who pray bring about a filling of the Spirit in the most powerful way. Many ministers are not prayerful. But the absence of the presence of God cannot be hid. The disciples experienced the manifest presence of God when they prayed. Prayer made the presence of God fill the room. The whole house where they were was shaken.

> Now when all the people were baptized, it came to pass, that Jesus also being baptized, and praying, the heaven was opened, And the Holy Ghost descended in a bodily shape like a dove upon him, and a voice came from heaven, which said, Thou art my beloved Son; in thee I am well pleased.
>
> Luke 3:21-22

> And it came to pass about an eight days after these sayings, he took Peter and John and James, and went up into a mountain to pray. And as he prayed, the fashion of his countenance was altered, and his raiment was white and glistering. And, behold, there talked with him two men, which were Moses and Elias: Who appeared in glory, and spake of his decease which he should accomplish at Jerusalem.
>
> Luke 9:28-31

Jesus walked in the presence of God. Jesus experienced several manifestations of God's presence. Most of them had to do with His times of prayer. He experienced the manifest presence of God in the River Jordan and actually heard the voice of God. He experienced this when He prayed and whilst praying. He also experienced glory and presence when He went up to the mountain to pray!

6. Those who obey God have the presence of God with them.

> And he that sent me is with me: the Father hath not left me alone; for I do always those things that please him.
>
> John 8:29

Jesus said that He experienced the presence of God continually because He ALWAYS obeyed God. Jesus always pleased God! Obedience to the will of God is the master key to walking in a continual presence of God. Do you want to experience the will of the Father? Decide to live a life that pleases God continually. Men of God who do not please God do not have the presence of God with them. They may be bishops, reverend ministers, pastors or anything else. But the presence of God may not be there. The mighty presence is a product of pleasing God.

Many men of God are living in disobedience. Many of us assume we know the will of God but are actually far from God. Disobedience to the call of God is the fast track route away from the presence of God. This is why you can see men of God quoting scriptures and speaking great words of wisdom but lacking the real presence of God. Samson lost the presence of God and did not even know it. In the same way many of us pastors do not even know that the presence of God is simply not there.

7. Those who ask for the presence of God have the presence of God.

And he said unto him, If thy presence go not with me, carry us not up hence. For wherein shall it be known here that I and thy people have found grace in thy sight? is it not in that thou goest with us? So shall we be separated, I and thy people, from all the people that are upon the face of the earth. And the Lord said unto Moses, I will do this thing also that thou hast spoken: for thou hast found grace in my sight, and I know thee by name.

Exodus 33:15-17

It is important to be conscious of the need for the presence of God. God's presence is what you need. Most people are concerned about their perfume or their make up or their outward appearance. What you need is the presence of God. Moses was very aware of the need to have God's presence. His prayers contained strong requests for the presence of God. He even told God he would not continue in the ministry without that presence.

Jesus taught us to ask for God's presence. He said it was the great and good gift that the Father would give to His children if they only asked for it. Let us begin to ask for the presence of God specifically. The Father is willing to let His presence be with us if we only learn to ask for it.

> If ye then, being evil, know how to give good gifts unto your children: how much more shall your heavenly Father give the Holy Spirit to them that ask him?
>
> Luke 11:13

Chapter 9

Serve in the Presence or out of the Presence

And again, whom should I serve? Should I not serve in the presence of his son? As I have served in thy father's presence, so will I be in thy presence.

2 Samuel 16:19

1. **You can serve God in His presence. You can also serve God outside His presence. These are two different experiences.**

   And Absalom said to Hushai, Is this thy kindness to thy friend? Why wentest thou not with thy friend?

   And Hushai said unto Absalom, Nay; but whom the Lord, and this people, and all the men of Israel, choose, his will I be, and with him will I abide. And again, whom should I serve? SHOULD I NOT SERVE IN THE PRESENCE OF HIS SON? AS I HAVE SERVED IN THY FATHER'S PRESENCE, SO WILL I BE IN THY PRESENCE.

   2 Samuel 16:17-19

   In the scripture above, Hushai the Archite deceived Absalom, the rebellious son with an amazing saying. In his speech, he revealed the significance of serving in the presence of the king. You see, Hushai had served in the government of Israel as an advisor to the king. To serve as an advisor to the king, he had to work in the very presence of the king. He knew what it meant to work in the presence of the king. Most people work outside the presence of the leader. They may work for the leader but outside his presence. Hushai reminded Absalom that he knew that it was a very great experience to work in the presence of the king. Anyone who has experienced working in the presence of the king would not like to work outside the presence of the king.

   I have quite a number of people that work for me in the ministry. However, just a few of these people work in my presence all the time. Even in my small world, I know that those who work in my presence have a higher and a nicer experience working than those who work outside my presence. This is exactly what it is like to serve God in His presence. It is much nicer and much higher to experience the presence of God as you work for God. Unfortunately, there are people who preach, teach and travel in the name of the Lord but are far away from the presence of the Lord. Through the teaching of this book, you must discover what the presence of God is and seek to serve God in His presence.

2. Serving in the presence of the king has great advantages.

And it came to pass in the month Nisan, in the twentieth year of Artaxerxes the king, that wine was before him: and I TOOK UP THE WINE, AND GAVE IT UNTO THE KING. Now I HAD NOT BEEN BEFORETIME SAD IN HIS PRESENCE.

Wherefore the king said unto me, why is thy countenance sad, seeing thou art not sick? this is nothing else but sorrow of heart. Then I was very sore afraid, And said unto the king, Let the king live for ever: why should not my countenance be sad, when the city, the place of my fathers' sepulchres, lieth waste, and the gates thereof are consumed with fire?

Then THE KING SAID UNTO ME, FOR WHAT DOST THOU MAKE REQUEST? So I prayed to the God of heaven.

Nehemiah 2:1-4

Nehemiah had the privilege of serving in the presence of the king Artaxerxes. Nehemiah enjoyed one of the great benefits of serving in the presence of the king. One day, the king noticed that his mood had changed. Do you think the king will notice that your mood has changed if you are not in his presence? Do you think the king would notice that you are not happy or that you need something if you are not in his presence?

When the king noticed that Nehemiah was unhappy, he asked him what his problem was. This interview with the king led to the great blessing of the rebuilding of the walls of Jerusalem by Nehemiah.

By being in the presence of the king, a great breakthrough was achieved. Great mercy, great kindness and great tenderness were shown to Nehemiah by the king. Obviously, the king was far greater than Nehemiah. He was in a completely different world.

Nehemiah was a slave, a captive. But he received great favour, just because his service was in the presence of the king. Indeed, you must seek to be a servant of God who serves in His presence.

3. **There is a beauty, a glory and an honour of serving in the presence of God as against serving in the church but not in His presence.**

   GLORY AND HONOUR ARE IN HIS PRESENCE; strength and gladness are in his place.

   1 Chronicles 16:27

   Notice that glory and the honour are found in the presence of the Lord. As you serve the Lord and His presence envelopes you, glory and honour will be yours. You will experience a certain beauty and a certain respect that only comes from the presence of the Lord.

4. **Even the trees notice the difference between serving in the presence and not serving in the presence of God.**

   Let the sea roar, and the fulness thereof: let the fields rejoice, and all that is therein. THEN SHALL THE TREES OF THE WOOD SING OUT AT THE PRESENCE OF THE LORD, because he cometh to judge the earth.

   O give thanks unto the Lord for he is good; for his mercy endureth for ever. And say ye, save us, O God of our salvation, and gather us together, and deliver us from the heathen, that we may give thanks to thy holy name, and glory in thy praise.

   1 Chronicles 16:32-35

   If you serve in the presence of God, supernatural things will happen all the time. Even the trees will sing! To serve in the presence of the Lord is to serve at very close quarters. Everything changes in the presence of God. The trees start singing when they are in the presence of God. It is time that you desire the presence of the Lord. Serve in His presence and enjoy a supernatural life!

Chapter 10

God's Presence in Secret Places

HE THAT DWELLETH IN THE SECRET PLACE OF THE MOST HIGH SHALL ABIDE UNDER THE SHADOW OF THE ALMIGHTY...HE SHALL COVER THEE WITH HIS FEATHERS, and under his wings shalt thou trust: his truth shall be thy shield and buckler... BECAUSE THOU HAST MADE THE LORD, which is my refuge, even the most High, THY HABITATION;

Psalms 91:1, 4, 9

God's presence is a mysterious experience that you can have when you are close to Him. Being close to God is the same as being in His presence. Being close to God is described in various mysterious ways. It is important that you grasp the mysterious descriptions that reveal that you are close to God. In the ninety-first Psalm, there are several mysterious descriptions of being close to God and therefore of being in His presence.

1. If you are in the secret place of the Most High, then you are close to God and you are in His presence. To be close to God is to be in the secret place of the Most High.
2. If you are under the shadow of the Most High, then you are close to God and you are in His presence. To be close to God is to dwell in the shadow of the Most High.
3. If you dwell under feathers of the Most High, then you are close to God and you are in His presence. To be close to God is to dwell under the feathers of the Lord.
4. If you make the Lord your refuge, then you are close to God and you are in His presence. To be close to God is to make God your refuge.
5. If you dwell in the habitation of the Most High, then you are close to God and you are in His presence. To be close to God is to dwell in His habitation.

Each of these close experiences will lead you to the presence of God. To be in the habitation of God and to be covered by His feathers is to be very close to God and to dwell in His presence. To live under the shadow of someone is to be extremely close to the person and therefore to experience his presence. The ninety-first Psalm is therefore a Psalm that describes the effect of staying close to God and staying in His presence. If indeed you are successful at staying under the shadow, the feathers, the habitation and the refuge of Almighty God, then you have succeeded in staying in His presence. Therefore, all the blessings of the presence of God are now yours because you are truly close to Him.

Notice the varied blessings that come upon those who enjoy His presence.

1. **The blessing of God's presence is security.**

   I will say of the Lord, HE IS MY REFUGE AND MY FORTRESS: my God; in him will I trust.

   Psalms 91:2

2. **The blessing of God's presence is deliverance from traps.**

   Surely HE SHALL DELIVER THEE FROM THE SNARE of the fowler, and from the noisome pestilence.

   Psalms 91:3

3. **The blessing of God's presence is deliverance from armed robbers by night and by day.**

   THOU SHALT NOT BE AFRAID FOR THE TERROR BY NIGHT; nor for the arrow that flieth by day; nor for the pestilence that walketh in darkness; nor for the destruction that wasteth at noonday.

   Psalms 91:5-6

4. **The blessing of God's presence is deliverance from plagues and epidemics.**

   THOU SHALT NOT BE AFRAID for the terror by night; nor for the arrow that flieth by day; nor FOR THE PESTILENCE that walketh in darkness; nor for the destruction that wasteth at noonday.

   Psalms 91:5-6

5. **The blessing of God's presence is divine escapes.**

   A thousand shall fall at thy side, and ten thousand at thy right hand; but it shall not come nigh thee.

   Psalms 91:7

6. **The blessing of God's presence is to attend funerals but not have your funeral, to visit the sick but not be visited as a sick person, to see evil but not to experience it.**

   Only with thine eyes shalt thou behold and see the reward of the wicked.

   Psalms 91:8

7. **The blessing of God's presence is continual angelic protection and angelic presence.**

   Because thou hast made the Lord, which is my refuge, even the most High, thy habitation; THERE SHALL NO EVIL BEFALL THEE, neither shall any plague come nigh thy dwelling.

   Psalms 91:9-10

8. **The blessing of God's presence is deliverance from natural disasters, natural phenomena, wild animals and accidents of nature.**

   Thou shalt tread upon the lion and adder: the young lion and the dragon shalt thou trample under feet.

   Psalms 91:13

9. **The blessing of God's presence is divine promotion.**

   Because he hath set his love upon me, therefore will I deliver him: I WILL SET HIM ON HIGH, because he hath known my name.

   Psalms 91:14

10. **The blessing of God's presence is divine deliverance.**

    He shall call upon me, and I will answer him: I will be with him in trouble; I WILL DELIVER him, and honour him.

    Psalms 91:15

11. The blessing of God's presence is divine honour.

He shall call upon me, and I will answer him: I will be with him in trouble; I WILL deliver him, and HONOUR HIM.

Psalms 91:15

12. The blessing of God's presence is the blessing of long life.

Because he hath set his love upon me, therefore will I deliver him: I will set him on high, because he hath known my name. He shall call upon me, and I will answer him: I will be with him in trouble; I will deliver him, and honour him. WITH LONG LIFE WILL I SATISFY HIM, and shew him my salvation.

Psalms 91:14-16

13. The blessing of God's presence is satisfaction and contentment.

Because he hath set his love upon me, therefore will I deliver him: I will set him on high, because he hath known my name. He shall call upon me, and I will answer him…

Psalms 91:14-15

14. The blessing of God's presence is that He will answer your prayers.

Because he hath set his love upon me, therefore will I deliver him: I will set him on high, because he hath known my name. HE SHALL CALL UPON ME, AND I WILL ANSWER HIM…

Psalms 91:14-15

15. The blessing of God's presence is the blessing of salvation.

Because he hath set his love upon me, therefore will I deliver him: I will set him on high, because he hath known my name. He shall call upon me, and I will answer him: I will be with him in trouble; I will deliver him, and honour him. With long life will I satisfy him, AND SHEW HIM MY SALVATION.

Psalms 91:14-16

Chapter 11

How You Can Enter the Presence of God With Thanksgiving

Enter into his gates with THANKSGIVING, and into his courts with PRAISE: BE THANKFUL unto him, and BLESS his name.

Psalms 100:4

1. The presence must be entered with thanksgiving.

You may approach God but you may not feel His presence. You may spend a long time praying but you may not feel His presence. It is important to know what to do in order to have the presence of God manifested in your life.

The presence of God will be enjoyed by those who are thankful. Thanksgiving is a master key to enjoying the presence of God. Saying "thank you" and being thankful are some of the most important spiritual virtues that you must develop if you are to enjoy the presence of God.

> O come, let us sing unto the Lord: let us make a joyful noise to the rock of our salvation. Let us COME BEFORE HIS PRESENCE WITH THANKSGIVING, and make a joyful noise unto him with psalms.
>
> Psalm 95:1-2

> ENTER INTO HIS GATES WITH THANKSGIVING, and into his courts with praise: be thankful unto him, and bless his name. For the Lord is good; his mercy is everlasting; and his truth endureth to all generations.
>
> Psalm 100:4-5

You will notice that being filled with the Spirit is predicated upon being thankful. Speaking psalms, hymns and spiritual songs are forms of giving thanks and praise to God. All through the New Testament, you will notice the exhortation to *be thankful* and to pray *with thanksgiving*. Thanksgiving ushers you directly into the presence of God. Being thankful and giving thanks is distinctly different from any other kind of prayer. When you are thankful, you have a good attitude, you have a grateful spirit and you have a pleasant disposition. These are attractive, even to human beings. They are also attractive to God. These attitudes, especially the posture of thankfulness, attracts the presence of God.

And be not drunk with wine, wherein is excess; but be filled with the Spirit; Speaking to yourselves in psalms and hymns and spiritual songs, singing and making melody in your heart to the Lord; GIVING THANKS ALWAYS for all things unto God and the Father in the name of our Lord Jesus Christ; Submitting yourselves one to another in the fear of God.

Ephesians 5:18-21

2. The presence of God is lost by being unthankful.

The opposite is also true. Being unthankful attracts evil spirits and drives away the presence of God. When you are unthankful, you drive God away. When you are unthankful, you drive away good people who love you and want to help you. No one wants to continue being nice to someone who is unthankful. Ungrateful people are the most unattractive people. They repel good company and drive away the very people that they need. The presence of God is dismissed by the attitude of unthankfulness.

Because that which may be known of God is manifest in them; for God hath shewed it unto them. For the invisible things of him from the creation of the world are clearly seen, being understood by the things that are made, even his eternal power and Godhead; so that they are without excuse: BECAUSE THAT, WHEN THEY KNEW GOD, THEY GLORIFIED HIM NOT AS GOD, NEITHER WERE THANKFUL; but became vain in their imaginations, and their foolish heart was darkened. Professing themselves to be wise, they became fools, And changed the glory of the uncorruptible God into an image made like to corruptible man, and to birds, and fourfooted beasts, and creeping things.

WHEREFORE GOD ALSO GAVE THEM UP to uncleanness through the lusts of their own hearts, to dishonour their own bodies between themselves:

Romans 1:19-24

In the scripture above, human beings lose the presence of God because of their unthankfulness. When human beings fail to glorify God and give Him thanks, they drive away the presence of God. Today, huge sections of Europe and America do not acknowledge God, do not praise God, do not glorify God and are not thankful to God. Because of this, the presence of God has departed from Europe and large parts of America. Even when they discovered wonderful details about the planets and the stars, human beings did not glorify God or praise Him or thank Him. Because of this, God gave them up and removed His presence. Today, the presence of God can hardly be found in some of these advanced European countries. When the presence of God departed from Europe, the continent was overrun by various perversions. When the presence of God is taken away, you are exposed to other strong spiritual forces that rush in.

When the Israelites were delivered from Egypt with mighty signs and wonders, they were not thankful. They were ungrateful to God in spite of all the miracles He had done for them. They lost the presence of God and evil spirits invaded them. The opposite of being thankful is complaining and murmuring. When the Israelites complained and murmured, evil spirits invaded their ranks. They were destroyed by several plagues, diseases and evils. It is important to maintain a thankful spirit when you want to maintain the presence of God. It is important to maintain a positive, thankful attitude if you are to have the presence of God.

NEITHER MURMUR YE, AS SOME OF THEM ALSO MURMURED, AND WERE DESTROYED of the destroyer. Now all these things happened unto them for examples: and they are written for our admonition, upon whom the ends of the world are come.

1 Corinthians 10:10-11

Chapter 12

How You Can Enter the Presence of God With Praise

Enter into his gates with thanksgiving, and INTO HIS COURTS WITH PRAISE: be thankful unto him, and BLESS HIS NAME.

Psalms 100:4

The presence of God is brought about through praise. Praise and worship is the secret that the modern church has learned. In former times, there was not much praise and worship. Many do not know that praise and worship, as we know it today, was not always practised in church. Many churches were dry and stiff, singing hymns at particular moments in the service.

The power of praise and worship has been rediscovered, especially in its ability to bring down the presence of God. There are many promises about how God will answer prayers. But there are not so many promises about how God will answer praises. Because of this, Christians did not know the power and effect of praises. Today, praise is offered in churches instead of prayer. The side effect of this is that many churches have become prayerless. There is no doubt that praise and worship have an almost miraculous way of bringing the presence of God into a church service.

Singing has an amazing way of bringing in the presence of God. Notice the scripture: "Come into His presence with singing."

Make a joyful noise unto the Lord, all ye lands. Serve the Lord with gladness: COME BEFORE HIS PRESENCE WITH SINGING.

Psalm 100:1-2

A man had the opportunity to be married at different times, to two different Christian ladies. For one of them, he was never sure what she was thinking when she came into his presence. Was she thinking of something bad or was she thinking of something good. The second wife, however, was a cheerful sister who seemed happy about everything. She would often come into his presence singing and excited. One day he was asked, "Which of the two wives made you happier?"

He answered, "Of course the second one was far more enjoyable. She welcomed me with singing, with joy and happiness. The first one was often moody and I was never sure of whether she was upset about something or not."

God equally enjoys His children coming to Him with singing, with thanksgiving and praises. If you want to experience the presence of God, you must learn to be thankful and full of praises when you come to God. You may approach God but you may not feel His presence until you learn to be full of singing, praise and thankfulness.

When Paul and Silas were in prison, they probably felt God had abandoned them. They did not sense the presence of God. But they sang praises at midnight and suddenly the presence of God appeared around them. There was a great earthquake and all the doors of the prison swung open.

And at midnight Paul and Silas prayed, and sang praises unto God: and the prisoners heard them. And suddenly there was a great earthquake, so that the foundations of the prison were shaken: and immediately all the doors were opened, and every one's bands were loosed.
Acts 16:25-26

Such is the power of praise, to bring the presence of God into your situation. Do not underestimate the power of praise when it comes to experiencing the presence of God.

Chapter 13

How to Enter the Presence of God By Being Upright

Surely the righteous shall give thanks unto thy name: THE UPRIGHT SHALL DWELL IN THY PRESENCE.

Psalms 140:13

You can continually stay in the presence of God by being upright. Your righteousness guarantees you the experience of the presence of God. As human beings, we do not stay in the presence of people who hate us, dislike us or gossip about us. God also does not stay in the presence of people who hate Him, who disobey Him and who fight Him constantly. The presence of God is for those who are in tune with God and who like Him very much. When you live an upright life, God has respect for you and He will dwell with you.

> **Behold, the Lord's hand is not shortened, that it cannot save; neither his ear heavy, that it cannot hear: But YOUR INIQUITIES HAVE SEPARATED BETWEEN YOU AND YOUR GOD, and your sins have hid his face from you, that he will not hear.**
> **Isaiah 59:1-2**

As you can see from this scripture, sin brings a big separation between you and God. That is why the presence of God goes away from you when you sin. Indeed, it is the upright who enjoy the presence of God. Most of our sins have to do with pride or the flesh. It is important that you humble yourself before God if you want to experience the presence of God. Flesh and pride cannot be exalted in the presence of God. No flesh can glory in His presence. Fleshliness is not wanted in the presence of God. You must get rid of the sins of flesh and the sins of pride if you want to experience the presence of God.

> **But God hath chosen the foolish things of the world to confound the wise; and God hath chosen the weak things of the world to confound the things which are mighty; And base things of the world, and things which are despised, hath God chosen, yea, and things which are not, to bring to nought things that are: That NO FLESH SHOULD GLORY IN HIS PRESENCE.**
> **1 Corinthians 1:27-29**

Many people have lost the presence of God because of sins of the flesh and sins of pride. If you are experienced, you will notice many great ministers of God who speak wonderful words and the principles of wisdom. However, if you are tuned to the Spirit, you will soon notice that some of them do not have the presence of God about them. They lack the presence of God because of the sins of pride and the sins of the flesh.

The presence of God is quite easy to detect when you know what it is like. Get tuned into the Spirit and start noticing people who still have the presence of God with them.

Chapter 14

Where there is Pride the Presence of God Leaves

Oh HOW GREAT IS THY GOODNESS, WHICH THOU HAST LAID UP FOR THEM THAT FEAR THEE; which thou hast wrought for them that trust in thee before the sons of men! THOU SHALT HIDE THEM IN THE SECRET OF THY PRESENCE FROM THE PRIDE OF MAN: thou shalt keep them secretly in a pavilion from the strife of tongues.

Psalms 31:19-20

God's presence is not found just anywhere. The secret of God's presence is that God hides His beautiful presence and glory away from the pride and wickedness of men. God is in no hurry to reveal Himself to wicked men. Sometimes it looks like if you were to explain more, speak more and share more, people would change. But you may even give your arm or your heart to your neighbour and he still will not repent. God has no time for the wickedness of man. He absolutely rejects the wickedness of man.

When Jesus Christ came to this world and showed the world God's power and glory, what did they do to Him? They crowned Him with thorns. They mocked Him and said, "You are a king who deserves to be crowned with nothing other than thorns." This is how wicked human beings are. That is why Jesus did not bother to do some of His greatest miracles in front of wicked men who would still not have believed any way.

He raised Jairus' daughter in the presence of her parents, Peter, James and John. He left out the wicked multitude because they did not deserve to see the greatness of God. He walked on water in front of His disciples. He was transfigured in front of Peter, James and John. All these were done privately. He would often tell people He healed, "Don't tell anyone." Indeed, the presence of God is hid from the pride of man.

1. Ezekiel experienced the presence of God away from the pride of man:

And the hand of the Lord was there upon me; and he said unto me, ARISE, GO FORTH INTO THE PLAIN, AND I WILL THERE TALK WITH THEE.

Then I AROSE, AND WENT FORTH INTO THE PLAIN: AND, BEHOLD, THE GLORY OF THE LORD STOOD THERE, as the glory which I saw by the river of Chebar: and I fell on my face. Then the spirit entered into me, and set me upon my feet, and spake with me, and said unto me, Go, shut thyself within thine house.

Ezekiel 3:22-24

God asked Ezekiel to go to a place where He would meet him and minister to him. When Ezekiel went to the plain, he saw the glory of God. He encountered the presence of God in a marvelous way and the Spirit entered into him.

2. Jacob experienced the presence of God away from the pride of man:

And Jacob awaked out of his sleep, and he said, SURELY THE LORD IS IN THIS PLACE; AND I KNEW IT NOT. And he was afraid, and said, How dreadful is this place! This is none other but the house of God, and this is the gate of heaven.

Genesis 28:16-17

Our religious training has made us understand that God is omnipotent, omnipresent and omniscient. This means that He is everywhere, He is all powerful and He knows everything. This is true. However, this religious mindset has made Christians think that God is equally present everywhere. God's presence is not equally distributed all over the world. There are places on earth where God's presence can be felt in a greater way. It is true that He is everywhere but it is your duty to find out where God's presence is and go there. Indeed, as you grow in your spiritual walk, you will see God direct you to the places where His presence is.

Jacob discovered this when he went to Bethel. He found out that God was present at Bethel in an unusual way. He said, "God is here and I did not even know it." The Bible is full of examples of this truth. Let us go through several of these amazing examples of how God instructs His people to find His presence in particular places. You will therefore find God asking His servants to meet Him at specific places. If God was simply omnipresent, He would meet people anywhere and it would not matter where He was meeting them. But consistently, you find God asking His servants to go to particular places in order to find His presence.

3. The Israelites experienced the presence of God away from the pride of man:

> TAKE HEED TO THYSELF THAT THOU OFFER NOT THY BURNT OFFERINGS IN EVERY PLACE THAT THOU SEEST: BUT IN THE PLACE WHICH THE LORD SHALL CHOOSE in one of thy tribes, there thou shalt offer thy burnt offerings, and there thou shalt do all that I command thee.
>
> Deuteronomy 12:13-14

God asked the children of Israel not to put their offerings or to worship just anywhere but where the Lord chose and appointed for them. The Lord had specific places where He wanted them to worship and present sacrifices. He warned them not to perform the sacrifice just anywhere. If God was equally everywhere, why would He warn them not to sacrifice at certain places?

> Thou shalt therefore sacrifice the passover unto the Lord thy God, of the flock and the herd, in the place which the Lord shall choose to place his name there. . . But at THE PLACE WHICH THE LORD THY GOD SHALL CHOOSE TO PLACE HIS NAME in, there thou shalt sacrifice the passover at even, at the going down of the sun, at the season that thou camest forth out of Egypt.
>
> Deuteronomy 16:2, 6

Over and over, the Lord emphasized that He would choose the place that they would celebrate the Passover and celebrate feasts. The Lord did not want them to have their spiritual encounters just anywhere.

> SEVEN DAYS SHALT THOU KEEP A SOLEMN FEAST UNTO THE LORD THY GOD IN THE PLACE WHICH THE LORD SHALL CHOOSE: because the Lord thy God shall bless thee in all thine increase, and in all the works of thine hands, therefore thou shalt surely rejoice.
> THREE TIMES IN A YEAR SHALL ALL THY MALES APPEAR BEFORE THE LORD THY GOD IN THE

PLACE WHICH HE SHALL CHOOSE; in the feast of unleavened bread, and in the feast of weeks, and in the feast of tabernacles: and they shall not appear before the Lord empty:

Deuteronomy 16:15-16

4. **The Mary Magdalene and the other Mary experienced the presence of God away from the pride of man:**

In the end of the Sabbath, as it began to dawn toward the first day of the week, came Mary Magdalene and the other Mary to see the sepulchre. And, behold, there was a great earthquake: for the angel of the Lord descended from heaven, and came and rolled back the stone from the door, and sat upon it ...

And the angel answered and said unto the women, Fear not ye: for I know that ye seek Jesus, which was crucified. He is not here: for he is risen, as he said. Come, see the place where the Lord lay. And go quickly, and tell his disciples that he is risen from the dead; and, behold, HE GOETH BEFORE YOU INTO GALILEE; THERE SHALL YE SEE HIM: lo, I have told you. And they departed quickly from the sepulchre with fear and great joy; and did run to bring his disciples word. And as they went to tell his disciples, behold, Jesus met them, saying, All hail. And they came and held him by the feet, and worshipped him. Then said Jesus unto them, Be not afraid: go tell my brethren THAT THEY GO INTO GALILEE, AND THERE SHALL THEY SEE ME.

Matthew 28:1-2, 5-10

Jesus and His disciples: Perhaps this is the most striking example of God specifying places where they would find His presence. Jesus asked His disciples to travel from Jerusalem to Galilee even though He could have met them anywhere. In this story, the angel told Mary to tell the disciples to go to Galilee to meet Him there. These two women carried on and actually met the Lord, Jesus, who gave the same instruction: "Tell the disciples to go to Galilee and I will meet them there." These ladies were in Jerusalem. Why didn't the Lord meet the disciples in Jerusalem if He could meet the ladies in Jerusalem? Why did they have to go all the way to Galilee in order to meet the Lord? I do not know why! What I do know is that God has special places where His presence is manifested. Your life is too short to wait to find out why certain things are so. You have to believe in appointed places of His presence so that you can experience more of the power and presence of God.

5. **The disciples experienced the presence of God away from the pride of man:**

> And, being assembled together with them, commanded them that THEY SHOULD NOT DEPART FROM JERUSALEM, BUT WAIT FOR THE PROMISE of the Father, which, saith he, ye have heard of me. For John truly baptized with water; but ye shall be baptized with the Holy Ghost not many days hence.
>
> Acts 1:4-5

> THEN RETURNED THEY UNTO JERUSALEM from the mount called Olivet, which is from Jerusalem a sabbath day's journey.
>
> Acts 1:12

Jesus then asked His disciples to come back from Galilee to wait in Jerusalem for the arrival of the Holy Spirit. This time, the place of appointment of the presence of God was Jerusalem. The presence of God kept moving around from Jerusalem to Galilee. It was up to the disciples to keep looking for the presence of God. Jerusalem and Galilee are about 200 kilometres apart. The Holy Spirit was going to fall in Jerusalem and not Galilee. Anyone who wanted to experience the Holy Spirit had to come to Jerusalem. Some would have asked, "Lord Jesus, please make up your mind where you want us to be." Some would have asked, "Are you not everywhere? Can you not just appear anywhere? In one moment you want us to be in Jerusalem. In the next moment you want us to be in Galilee."

6. Isaac experienced the presence of God away from the pride of man:

And the Lord appeared unto him, and said, GO NOT DOWN INTO EGYPT; DWELL IN THE LAND WHICH I SHALL TELL THEE OF: SOJOURN IN THIS LAND, and I will be with thee, and will bless thee; for unto thee, and unto thy seed, I will give all these countries, and I will perform the oath which I sware unto Abraham thy father; And I will make thy seed to multiply as the stars of heaven, and will give unto thy seed all these countries; and in thy seed shall all the nations of the earth be blessed; Because that Abraham obeyed my voice, and kept my charge, my commandments, my statutes, and my laws. And Isaac dwelt in Gerar:

Genesis 26:2-6

God chose Gerar for Isaac to stay and to prosper there. Supernatural prosperity was dependent on his staying in that location. God asked Isaac not to go to Egypt. He would not find the presence of God there. God had not chosen to bless Isaac in Egypt. When Isaac stayed in Gerar, we find that God blessed him so much that he became supernaturally and unusually great. The presence of God was manifested in the life of Isaac. This supernatural greatness was dependent upon Isaac not going to Egypt but rather staying in Gerar.

THEN ISAAC SOWED IN THAT LAND, and received in the same year an hundredfold: and the Lord blessed him. AND THE MAN WAXED GREAT, AND WENT FORWARD, AND GREW UNTIL HE BECAME VERY GREAT: For he had possession of flocks, and possession of herds, and great store of servants: and the Philistines envied him.

Genesis 26:12-14

7. Joseph experienced the presence of God away from the pride of man:

And JOSEPH WAS BROUGHT DOWN TO EGYPT; and Potiphar, an officer of Pharaoh, captain of the guard, an Egyptian, bought him of the hands of the Ishmeelites, which had brought him down thither. And THE LORD WAS WITH JOSEPH, and he was a prosperous man; and he was in the house of his master the Egyptian. And his master saw that THE LORD WAS WITH HIM, and that the Lord made all that he did to prosper in his hand.

Genesis 39:1-3

Joseph, on the other hand found the presence of God in Egypt. It was when he went down to Egypt and became a slave in Potiphar's house that the presence of God was manifested.

8. Naaman experienced the presence of God away from the pride of man:

The prophet Elisha gave Naaman a specific place to experience miracle healing. He told him that he would need to visit the River Jordan and bath in it seven times. Naaman was aghast. Why should I have to bath in the river Jordan? He protested at the idea of bathing in the Jordan because he knew of other rivers that he could bath in. He protested saying that the rivers Abana and Pharpar were better. I would not doubt that the river Abana and Pharpar may have been better than the river Jordan. The river Jordan has a very big name but it is in actual fact a very narrow river with muddy and murky water. It is not attractive at all and I, personally, would not relish the thought of going into that river. I can understand why Naaman balked at the idea of going into the river Jordan. But that is where God had chosen for His power to be manifested.

So Naaman came with his horses and with his chariot, and stood at the door of the house of Elisha. And Elisha sent a messenger unto him, saying, GO AND WASH IN JORDAN SEVEN TIMES, AND THY FLESH SHALL

COME AGAIN TO THEE, and thou shalt be clean. But Naaman was wroth, and went away, and said, Behold, I thought, He will surely come out to me, and stand, and call on the name of the Lord his God, and strike his hand over the place, and recover the leper. ARE NOT ABANA AND PHARPAR, RIVERS OF DAMASCUS, BETTER THAN ALL THE WATERS OF ISRAEL? MAY I NOT WASH IN THEM, AND BE CLEAN? So he turned and went away in a rage.

2 Kings 5:9-12

9. The pool of Bethesda enjoyed the presence of God away from the pride of man:

Now there is at Jerusalem by the sheep market a pool, which is called in the Hebrew tongue Bethesda, having five porches. In these lay a great multitude of impotent folk, of blind, halt, withered, waiting for the moving of the water. For an angel went down at a certain season into the pool, and troubled the water: whosoever then first after the troubling of the water stepped in was made whole of whatsoever disease he had.

John 5:2-4

The pool of Bethesda was where the Lord chose to do great miracles. Because of this, a multitude of sick people were always found around the pool. When the presence of God manifested, it was important to be the first to get into the pool. God had chosen Bethesda for great healings. Even Jesus performed one of His greatest miracles at the Pool of Bethesda. Like the multitude of sick people who recognized where the presence of God was, it is important that we recognize where the presence of God is and congregate there.

10. The land of Moriah experienced the presence of God away from the pride of man:

And it came to pass after these things, that God did tempt Abraham, and said unto him, Abraham: and he said,

> Behold, here I am. And he said, TAKE NOW THY SON, THINE ONLY SON ISAAC, WHOM THOU LOVEST, AND GET THEE INTO THE LAND OF MORIAH; AND OFFER HIM THERE FOR A BURNT OFFERING UPON ONE OF THE MOUNTAINS WHICH I WILL TELL THEE OF. And Abraham rose up early in the morning, and saddled his ass, and took two of his young men with him, and Isaac his son, and clave the wood for the burnt offering, and rose up, and went unto the place of which God had told him. Then on the third day Abraham lifted up his eyes, and saw the place afar off...
>
> The Angel of the Lord called to Abraham from heaven a second time And said, By myself have I sworn, saith the Lord, for because thou hast done this thing, and hast not withheld thy son, thine only son: That in blessing I will bless thee, and in multiplying I will multiply thy seed as the stars of the heaven, and as the sand which is upon the sea shore; and thy seed shall possess the gate of his enemies; and in thy seed shall all the nations of the earth be blessed; because thou hast obeyed my voice.
>
> Genesis 22:1-4, 15-18

The mountains of Moriah were chosen by God for Abraham's greatest blessing. You may think that God is unreasonable in asking a ninety-nine year old man to go mountain climbing. You can imagine how difficult it was for Abraham at his age to climb a mountain and scale over rocks. But God had appointed a specific place on the mount of Moriah where Abraham would be tested and receive the greatest blessing for himself and his descendants. It was on Mount Moriah that these great events were destined to take place. Abraham had no other option than to climb the mountain to seek the presence of God. I pray that you will have the humility and the energy to go to the places that God has appointed for your blessing.

11. Chorazin and Bethsaida experienced the presence of God away from the pride of man:

THEN BEGAN HE TO UPBRAID THE CITIES WHEREIN MOST OF HIS MIGHTY WORKS WERE DONE, because they repented not: Woe unto thee, Chorazin! woe unto thee, Bethsaida! for if the mighty works, which were done in you, had been done in Tyre and Sidon, they would have repented long ago in sackcloth and ashes.

Matthew 11:20-21

When you read the Bible, you get the feeling that Jesus performed thousands of miracles everywhere He went. A closer look at the ministry of Jesus shows that He did not do great miracles everywhere. Indeed there were places that the presence of God was manifested in a much greater way than others. Chorazin and Bethsaida were chosen by the Lord for the manifestation of great miracles. Other places did not experience such miracles.

Chapter 15

The Presence of God is Mysterious

And Jacob awaked out of his sleep, and he said, Surely the Lord is in this place; and I knew it not.

Genesis 28:16

The presence and glory of God is indeed a mysterious topic. Do not expect to have three simple steps that describe the awesome glory and presence of God. At best, you can expect a mystical or not-so-clear discussion on what the presence and glory of God actually is.

1. The presence of God is a mystery.

It is His presence that makes you see His glory, His beauty and His majesty. There are things in the word of God that are intentionally unclear. Jesus spoke to the multitudes in parables. He intentionally kept the mysteries of God from their undeserving ears.

When Lazarus died, Jesus spoke mystically to His disciples saying that Lazarus was asleep. This was intentional. At a later stage, Jesus spoke plainly to His disciple and said that Lazarus is dead.

THEN SAID JESUS unto them PLAINLY, Lazarus is dead.

John 11:14

This shows that at a point Jesus did not intend to make things clear. Do not expect a clear and easy-to-understand teaching about the presence and the glory of God. Expect to enjoy the mysteries of God.

> And he said, My presence shall go with thee, and I will give thee rest. And he said unto him, IF THY PRESENCE GO NOT WITH ME, CARRY US NOT UP HENCE. For wherein shall it be known here that I and thy people have found grace in thy sight? is it not in that thou goest with us? so shall we be separated, I and thy people, from all the people that are upon the face of the earth.
>
> And the Lord said unto Moses, I will do this thing also that thou hast spoken: for thou hast found grace in my sight, and I know thee by name. AND HE SAID, I BESEECH THEE, SHEW ME THY GLORY. AND HE SAID, I

WILL MAKE ALL MY GOODNESS PASS BEFORE THEE, and I will proclaim the name of the Lord before thee; and will be gracious to whom I will be gracious, and will shew mercy on whom I will shew mercy. And he said, Thou canst not see my face: for there shall no man see me, and live.

Exodus 33:14-20

2. The presence of God is compatible with helpers.

Whilst in the presence of God a helper was allowed to be there without departing and his presence was not seen as a distraction or something wrong. There are some people who are compatible with the presence of God. They are servants and their presence does not destroy the awesome times of fellowship with the Holy Spirit.

And it came to pass, as Moses entered into the tabernacle, the cloudy pillar descended, and stood at the door of the tabernacle, and the Lord talked with Moses. And all the people saw the cloudy pillar stand at the tabernacle door: and all the people rose up and worshipped, every man in his tent door.

AND THE LORD SPAKE UNTO MOSES FACE TO FACE, AS A MAN SPEAKETH UNTO HIS FRIEND. AND HE TURNED AGAIN INTO THE CAMP: BUT HIS SERVANT JOSHUA, THE SON OF NUN, A YOUNG MAN, DEPARTED NOT OUT OF THE TABERNACLE.

Exodus 33:9-11

3. Ordinary people do not want the presence of God.

Ordinary people often just want the benefits of God. They do not want to come near God Himself. They want Him to give them money, husbands and promotion. They do not want all that prayer stuff and they do not want to be spiritual. This is exactly what happened with Moses and the Israelites. The people said, "You speak with him, we do not want to speak with Him. You deal with Him and bless us afterwards."

These words the Lord spake unto all your assembly in the mount out of the midst of the fire, of the cloud, and of the thick darkness, with a great voice: and he added no more. And he wrote them in two tables of stone, and delivered them unto me. And it came to pass, when ye heard the voice out of the midst of the darkness, (for the mountain did burn with fire,) that ye came near unto me, even all the heads of your tribes, and your elders; And ye said, Behold, the Lord our God hath shewed us his glory and his greatness, and we have heard his voice out of the midst of the fire: we have seen this day that God doth talk with man, and he liveth.

Now therefore why should we die? for this great fire will consume us: if we hear the voice of the Lord our God any more, then we shall die. FOR WHO IS THERE OF ALL FLESH, THAT HATH HEARD THE VOICE OF THE LIVING GOD SPEAKING OUT OF THE MIDST OF THE FIRE, AS WE HAVE, AND LIVED? GO THOU NEAR, AND HEAR ALL THAT THE LORD OUR GOD SHALL SAY: AND SPEAK THOU UNTO US ALL THAT THE LORD OUR GOD SHALL SPEAK UNTO THEE; AND WE WILL HEAR IT, AND DO IT.

Deuteronomy 5:22-27

Knowing God and His presence helps you to know His ways and not just His acts. His acts are the manifestations and deeds. Many people know His acts but do not know Him as a person.

> He made known his ways unto Moses, his acts unto the children of Israel.
>
> Psalm 103:7

4. The presence of God is experienced by consecrated people.

AND THE LORD SAID UNTO MOSES, GO UNTO THE PEOPLE, AND SANCTIFY THEM TO DAY AND TO MORROW, AND LET THEM WASH THEIR CLOTHES,

AND BE READY AGAINST THE THIRD DAY: FOR THE THIRD DAY THE LORD WILL COME DOWN IN THE SIGHT OF ALL THE PEOPLE UPON MOUNT SINAI. And thou shalt set bounds unto the people round about, saying, Take heed to yourselves, that ye go not up into the mount, or touch the border of it: whosoever toucheth the mount shall be surely put to death: There shall not an hand touch it, but he shall surely be stoned, or shot through; whether it be beast or man, it shall not live: when the trumpet soundeth long, they shall come up to the mount. And Moses went down from the mount unto the people, and sanctified the people; and they washed their clothes. And he said unto the people, be ready against the third day: come not at your wives. And it came to pass on the third day in the morning, that there were thunders and lightnings, and a thick cloud upon the mount, and the voice of the trumpet exceeding loud; so that all the people that was in the camp trembled.

Exodus 19:10-16

5.   The presence of God is experienced by those not contaminated with women.

And the Lord said unto Moses, Go unto the people, and sanctify them to day and to morrow, and let them wash their clothes, And be ready against the third day: for the third day the Lord will come down in the sight of all the people upon mount Sinai. And thou shalt set bounds unto the people round about, saying, Take heed to yourselves, that ye go not up into the mount, or touch the border of it: whosoever toucheth the mount shall be surely put to death: There shall not an hand touch it, but he shall surely be stoned, or shot through; whether it be beast or man, it shall not live: when the trumpet soundeth long, they shall come up to the mount.

And Moses went down from the mount unto the people, and sanctified the people; and they washed their clothes.

And he said unto the people, Be ready against the third day: COME NOT AT YOUR WIVES. And it came to pass on the third day in the morning, that there were thunders and lightnings, and a thick cloud upon the mount, and the voice of the trumpet exceeding loud; so that all the people that was in the camp trembled.

Exodus 19:10-16

Do not come near your wives if you want to see the presence of God! This was the instruction given to the Israelites. If you want to see God's presence, stay away from your wives.

And I looked, and, lo, a Lamb stood on the mount Sion, and with him an hundred forty and four thousand, having his Father's name written in their foreheads. And I heard a voice from heaven, as the voice of many waters, and as the voice of a great thunder: and I heard the voice of harpers harping with their harps: And they sung as it were a new song before the throne, and before the four beasts, and the elders: and no man could learn that song but the hundred and forty and four thousand, which were redeemed from the earth. THESE ARE THEY WHICH WERE NOT DEFILED WITH WOMEN; FOR THEY ARE VIRGINS. These are they which follow the Lamb whithersoever he goeth. These were redeemed from among men, being the firstfruits unto God and to the Lamb. And in their mouth was found no guile: for they are without fault before the throne of God.

Revelation 14:1-5

Notice that it is the absence of sin, the consecration of the people and the absence of the defilement by women that led to the presence of God. What is the defilement of women? Is it a sin to be married? No! So what is it about women that defiles? The defilement of women is caused by the turning away of the hearts of God's people from following after Him to loving women.

God can use your whole life to rid you of any love or affection that you have for anything other than Him. God is number one!

He will not share His position with your sweetheart, no matter how sweet she is!

Many people, blessed with good marriages, have forsaken their true ministry in exchange for holding on to their blissful relationships. God is not against blissful relationships but He is against any relationship that makes Him number two.

Chapter 16

The Presence of God and Prosperity

And THE LORD WAS WITH JOSEPH, AND HE WAS A PROSPEROUS MAN; and he was in the house of his master the Egyptian.

Genesis 39:2

The Bible is full of examples of people who enjoyed the presence of God and its attendant prosperity. *God's presence creates prosperity.* This is one of the reasons why we must stay close to God. It makes sense to think that someone who is close to the king will have access to some of the wealth and riches that the king enjoys. This is why people are happy when their friend or acquaintance becomes the president of a country. The riches and power that their friend comes into, by virtue of his being the head of state, will surely affect them. Every king has friends and every king has people that secretly enjoy the wealth and prosperity of the throne.

Mordecai was such a person. He came out of the king's presence completely overloaded with riches, wealth, promotion and prosperity.

> And MORDECAI WENT OUT FROM THE PRESENCE OF THE KING IN ROYAL APPAREL of blue and white, and with a great crown of gold, and with a garment of fine linen and purple: and the city of Shushan rejoiced and was glad.
> The Jews had light, and gladness, and joy, and honor. And in every province, and in every city, whithersoever the king's commandment and his decree came, the Jews had joy and gladness, a feast and a good day. And many of the people of the land became Jews; for the fear of the Jews fell upon them.
>
> Esther 8:15-17

Mordecai's experience of coming out of the king's presence fully loaded with prosperity will be your portion as you seek to experience the presence of God in your life and ministry. When the presence of God fades away, the power of God that gives rise to genuine prosperity is gone. Struggles and difficulties replace noiseless rent-free prosperity.

Rent-free prosperity is the kind of prosperity that people have when they do not have to make monthly payments for anything; whether it is a loan or a mortgage. Today, many people pretend to be prosperous but are actually drowning in debts. Any kind of shaking or change in the equilibrium will lead to devastation and crises. You will experience true prosperity when the presence of God is with you. There are some beautiful examples of this kind of spirit that comes from the presence of God.

1. Joseph the slave prospered because of the presence of God:

> And Joseph was brought down to Egypt; and Potiphar, an officer of Pharaoh, captain of the guard, an Egyptian, bought him of the hands of the Ishmaelites, which had brought him down thither.
>
> And THE LORD WAS WITH JOSEPH, AND HE WAS A PROSPEROUS MAN; and he was in the house of his master the Egyptian. And his master saw that the Lord was with him, and that the Lord made all that he did to prosper in his hand. And Joseph found grace in his sight, and he served him: and he made him overseer over his house, and all that he had he put into his hand.
>
> Genesis 39:1-4

The scripture is quite clear on the source of Joseph's prosperity. The Lord was with him! The presence of God was with Joseph and he prospered even when he was a slave. Today, people who are free cannot prosper in the same way that Joseph prospered when he was slave. God was with Joseph and that is why he prospered as a slave. God was with Joseph and that is why he prospered in prison.

2. Joseph the prisoner prospered because of the presence of God:

> And it came to pass, when his master heard the words of his wife, which she spake unto him, saying, After this manner did thy servant to me; that his wrath was kindled. And Joseph's master took him, and put him into the prison, a place where the king's prisoners were bound: and he was there in the prison.

BUT THE LORD WAS WITH JOSEPH, AND SHEWED HIM MERCY, AND GAVE HIM FAVOUR in the sight of the keeper of the prison. And the keeper of the prison committed to Joseph's hand all the prisoners that were in the prison; and whatsoever they did there, he was the doer of it. The keeper of the prison looked not to any thing that was under his hand; BECAUSE THE LORD WAS WITH HIM, AND THAT WHICH HE DID, THE LORD MADE IT TO PROSPER.

Genesis 39:19-23

You will notice how Joseph prospered as a prisoner. People who are walking about freely are not able to experience the prosperity that Joseph experienced. The reason for Joseph's prosperity is written clearly in the Bible: "The Lord was with him!"

You must believe that prosperity is directly linked to the presence of God. Today, many ministers claim to be teaching prosperity but actually have nothing. There are people who have metamorphosed from being genuine pastors and evangelists into being motivational speakers all in the effort to get more money.

People have thought that changing the message of the gospel into one of prosperity would lead to wealth. Unfortunately, most of these efforts have not led to prosperity. The fruits of these financial, business, motivational, and market place ministries have been to turn the church into a materialistic and lukewarm church. Today, many Christians no longer love God but seek wealth. There can be no greater perversion of the gospel than this unfortunate emphasis on materialism. As a result of this, the church is left in weakness and poverty, unable to build church buildings, unable to have crusades and unable to reach out to the lost.

The presence of God departs from anyone who departs from the commandment of God. Therefore, the prosperity of God also departs from those who shift away from building churches and evangelising the world as Jesus asked us to. Note this important scripture about obeying God:

> Jesus answered and said unto him, If a man love me, he will keep my words: and my Father will love him, and we will come unto him, and make our abode with him.
>
> John 14:23

From this scripture, we see that obeying God causes God's presence to come to be with us. This means that obeying God will lead eventually to prosperity. When God is with you, as He was with Joseph, you will experience prosperity. What are the commandments of God? The commandments of God are to love God, to preach the gospel, to go witnessing and to build churches. Meditate on these things and you will discover that there is no greater task that God has given to us than to reach the world for Jesus Christ.

This is why Matthew 28:19-20 is called the Great Commission and the Great Commandment. The commandment to go into the world and preach the gospel, towers above all other commandments that Jesus gave. It is when we obey His last and greatest command that we can say we have fulfilled the greatest commandment which is to love God. Let us strive to regain the presence of God that is lost to the church. The television is full of debt-ridden pastors in financial crises begging for money and over-emphasising on giving and receiving.

Desire the presence of God and experience the presence of God and you will prosper whether you are a slave or a prisoner. If Joseph prospered in prison, you can prosper as a free man. All you need is the presence of God. I know that to some people this may sound simplistic. You can argue with me but you cannot argue with the word of God.

3. Isaac prospered because of the presence of God:

And the Lord appeared unto him, and said, Go not down into Egypt; dwell in the land which I shall tell thee of: Sojourn in this land, and I WILL BE WITH THEE, AND WILL BLESS THEE; for unto thee, and unto thy seed, I will give all these countries, and I will perform the oath which I sware unto Abraham thy father; And I will make thy seed to multiply as the stars of heaven, and will give unto thy seed all these countries; and in thy seed shall all the nations of the earth be blessed; Because that Abraham obeyed my voice, and kept my charge, my commandments, my statutes, and my laws. And Isaac dwelt in Gerar:

Genesis 26:2-6

Then Isaac sowed in that land, and received in the same year an hundredfold: and the Lord blessed him. AND THE MAN WAXED GREAT, AND WENT FORWARD, AND GREW UNTIL HE BECAME VERY GREAT: For he had possession of flocks, and possession of herds, and great store of servants: and the Philistines envied him.

Genesis 26:12-14

Isaac is famous for being the one that waxed great, went forward and grew until he became very great. But he did not just suddenly become very great. The Lord had promised His presence to Isaac. "Sojourn in this land, and I will be with thee and bless thee." All you need is the presence of God. Isaac was promised the presence of God and that was enough to make him prosper in a poverty-stricken and cursed place. Decide to live where God asks you to live!

4. Obededom prospered because of the presence of God:

So David would not remove the ark of the Lord unto him into the city of David: but David carried it aside into the house of Obededom the Gittite. And The ark of the lord continued in the house of Obededom the Gittite three months: and the Lord blessed Obededom, and all his household.

AND IT WAS TOLD KING DAVID, SAYING, THE LORD HATH BLESSED THE HOUSE OF OBEDEDOM, AND ALL THAT PERTAINETH UNTO HIM, BECAUSE OF THE ARK OF GOD. So David went and brought up the ark of God from the house of Obededom into the city of David with gladness.

2 Samuel 6:10-12

Obededom is another character that experienced prosperity because of the presence of the Lord. The reason for his prosperity is clear. The ark of God in his house made everything in his house to prosper. He experienced great prosperity because of the ark and not because of his profession or his hard work. Most people think they experience prosperity because of their hard work or their many degrees. The presence of God will change your level of prosperity.

Chapter 17

Obedience: the Master Key to The Presence of God

And HE THAT SENT ME IS WITH ME: the Father hath not left me alone; FOR I DO ALWAYS THOSE THINGS THAT PLEASE HIM.

John 8:29

1. **Behold, I GO FORWARD, BUT HE IS NOT THERE; and BACKWARD, BUT I CANNOT PERCEIVE HIM: ON THE LEFT HAND, where he doth work, but I CANNOT BEHOLD HIM: he hideth himself ON THE RIGHT HAND, that I CANNOT SEE HIM: But he knoweth the way that I take: when he hath tried me, I shall come forth as gold. My foot hath held his steps, his way have I kept, and not declined.**

   Neither have I gone back from the commandment of his lips; I HAVE ESTEEMED THE WORDS OF HIS MOUTH MORE THAN MY NECESSARY FOOD.

   Job 23:8-12

This amazing scripture reveals how Job was searching for the presence of God. He went forward, backward and did many things to find the presence of God. However, he was not able to find the presence of God until he gave himself to the commandments of God. You cannot easily see God and you cannot easily find His presence until you esteem the word of God more importantly than your necessary food.

2. **And HE THAT SENT ME IS WITH ME: the Father hath not left me alone; FOR I DO ALWAYS THOSE THINGS THAT PLEASE HIM.**

   John 8:29

Obedience to God is even more important than entering His gates with thanksgiving. Most Christians attempt to enter the gate with thanksgiving but are soon prevented from the presence of God. The presence of God is with you because you do the things that please Him. Obedience is key if you want to experience the presence of God continually.

Let's be serious! Let's be honest! You would not entertain people in your presence that were not obedient to you. We all keep our most obedient followers close to our side. Many men marry the girl that is most submissive and obedient to them. I married the lady that was most submissive and obedient to me. Obedience is extremely attractive and it draws your superiors into your life like a strong magnet that is attracting metal shavings.

Almighty God is equally attracted to His obedient servants. Many people sing praise and worship and enter His gates and His courts. Unfortunately, soon after entering the courts, they are asked to leave because they are recognised as dangerous and disobedient rebels. A disobedient person is a dangerous person. A disobedient person is stubborn and rebellious against your wishes and ideas. A disobedient person can turn into a "Judas" and betray you. No wonder God does not entertain disobedient people in His presence. God does not give His presence to those who are disobedient.

Today, large parts of the church are stricken with poverty and an inability to do anything substantial for the Lord. This is very ironic because most of the church is preaching about money, prosperity, general improvement and happiness. Yet the church is riddled with debts, mortgages and insolvency.

Jesus gave the reason why God's presence was with Him. He said clearly that the Father was with Him because He was constantly doing the things that pleased the Father. What are the things that will please the Father today? The things that will please the Father are the things that are written in the Bible.

Jesus said in Matthew 16, "I will build my church and the gates of hell will not prevail against it." The only project I know that Jesus is doing is building His church. Why not please Jesus and join Him in what He has declared that He is doing – building the church? Instead of building the church, many of us are building businesses, schools, hospitals, universities and other good things. None of these things are evil in themselves. But they are cleverly and satanically deceptive when they take us away from the main thing.

Satan is too intelligent to give church leaders evil things to do. He only gives good things to church leaders to do. However, the good things that satan gives us to do are a complete distraction from our actual job of winning the lost, preaching the gospel and building the church. The first commandment was, "Follow me I will make you fishers of men." What could be more emphatic and clear for us to do than to go into the world and make fishers of men?

If you are discerning, you will notice that the presence of God is not with many people who are preaching and leading the church down the road of materialism and secularism. "Go ye into all the world and preach the gospel" is not a human idea. It is God's word! Today, human philosophies and big English words are preached in place of God's word.

Please be careful of people who preach human philosophies laced with scriptures. It is as though some ministers have decided to tickle the fancies of men and give mental pleasures to their listeners rather than preaching the word of God. Remember the words of Jesus Christ: "My father is with me because I always do the things that please him." Obeying God and obeying the Father is essential for maintaining the presence of the Father in your life.

3. **Jesus answered and said unto him, IF A MAN love me, he will KEEP MY WORDS: and my Father will love him, and WE WILL COME UNTO HIM, AND MAKE OUR ABODE WITH HIM.**

John 14:23

In this landmark scripture, Jesus promises that He and the Father would come and manifest themselves to you in a special way because you keep His commandments. Is that not what we all seek for, the manifestation of God in our lives and ministries? What are God's manifestations? The manifestation of God's power in your life is healing, deliverance, prosperity, blessings and every other supernatural empowerment and elevation that you can think of.

Supernatural empowerment and supernatural promotion only come from God. They are manifestations of God's power. As weak human beings we have sought to find all these things in our own way, using our own strength. Our own strength is failing miserably. The presence of God has many manifestations. It is time to seek the presence of God with all your heart so that you can experience the presence of God with all the manifestations in your life.

4. **Oh how great is thy goodness, which thou hast laid up for them that fear thee; which thou hast wrought for them that trust in thee before the sons of men! Thou shalt hide them IN THE SECRET OF THY PRESENCE FROM THE PRIDE OF MAN: thou shalt keep them secretly in a pavilion from the strife of tongues. Blessed be the Lord: for he hath shewed me his marvellous kindness in a strong city.**

Psalms 31:19-21

The secret of God's presence is hidden away from the pride of man. Today, many people in the ministry are interested in things that are simply the pride of man. The impressive cars, the impressive houses, the gold, the diamonds, the power, the influence, the impressions, the money, the politics and the fame are all of the pride of man. God's presence is not found where the pride of man is found. God's presence is found in humility and lowliness.

Moses was the meekest man on earth and he saw the presence of God like no other person ever has. Jesus Christ - "God with us", was born in a manger amongst animals. Satan was defeated because he could not comprehend how Almighty God would condescend to such a low estate. Do not seek to impress men. Do not seek to change the simple and humble gospel message into an impressive university lecture or into an impressive political speech with quotations from Henry Ford, Socrates or Plato.

The presence of God is not found in the pride of man. The presence of God is found in the humility of the great works of God. You will achieve much more for God by having His presence with you. Humble obedience is a master key to enjoying the presence of God.

5. **And the Lord said unto Moses, Depart, and go up hence, thou and the people which thou hast brought up out of the land of Egypt, unto the land which I sware unto Abraham, to Isaac, and to Jacob, saying, Unto thy seed will I give it: And I will send an angel before thee; and I will drive out the Canaanite, the Amorite, and the Hittite, and the Perizzite, the Hivite, and the Jebusite: Unto a land flowing with milk and honey: for I WILL NOT GO UP IN THE MIDST OF THEE; FOR THOU ART A STIFFNECKED PEOPLE: lest I consume thee in the way.**

Exodus 33:1-3

In this scripture, the Lord said He would no more be in the midst of the Israelites because they were stubborn. You lose the divine presence because of your stubbornness and resistance to instructions. Indeed, being stubborn, being resistant and being slow to obey will cause you to lose the presence of God.

Chapter 18

Benefits of the Presence of God

And he said, MY PRESENCE SHALL GO WITH THEE, AND I WILL GIVE THEE REST. And he said unto him, If thy presence go not with me, carry us not up hence.

Exodus 33:14

The presence of God has many benefits. All though the Bible, you see the importance of living in the presence of God and enjoying the effects of God being with you. In this chapter, I want us to go through some of the amazing benefits of the presence of God.

1. The presence of God gives rest all around.

> And he said, MY PRESENCE SHALL GO WITH THEE, AND I WILL GIVE THEE REST. And he said unto him, If thy presence go not with me, carry us not up hence.
>
> For wherein shall it be known here that I and thy people have found grace in thy sight? IS IT NOT IN THAT THOU GOEST WITH US? so shall we be separated, I and thy people, from all the people that are upon the face of the earth.
>
> Exodus 33:14-16

It's not worth going around without God's presence. Your struggles and your striving are evidence that you lack the presence of God. Where the presence of God is, there is rest and peace. God's presence takes care of many things. You will enjoy peace when you learn to abide in the presence of God. You will learn that it is God's power that works for you and gives you the victory.

2. The presence of the Lord brings refreshing.

> Repent ye therefore, and be converted, that your sins may be blotted out, when the times of REFRESHING shall come FROM THE PRESENCE OF THE LORD;
>
> Acts 3:19

When you feel refreshed it is because of the presence of the Lord. People who are stale and unable to walk in newness in ministry prove that they lack the presence of God. When someone ministers and you sense freshness, you are sensing the presence of God. When you go to church and come back feeling refreshed, it is because you experienced the presence of God.

When you go to church and feel dead, stale and dry, it is because you did not experience the presence of God. Perhaps, this is one of the easiest ways to detect the presence of God. It is something you must look out for in a ministry. Sometimes, when I watch ministers, I notice how they give beautiful illustrations, philosophies and even scriptures. It may be very logical and very convincing but somehow I do not sense a freshness and a refreshing that comes from the presence of God. That is how you know that the ministry is departed from the presence of God. It has ceased to bring a certain refreshing. I once listened to a great man of God teaching. I truly enjoyed his messages and searched for more of his preaching tapes. After a few years, however, I could not understand what he was preaching about any more. I gradually stopped listening to him and I could never re-establish that line of blessing till he died.

After he died, I found out that he criticized the preaching of the cross and the blood of Jesus. I was amazed as I listened to him ridiculing the all-important message of the cross and the blood of Jesus. I thought to myself, "Perhaps this is why I somehow didn't enjoy his ministry any more." At the time, I did not have a good reason. I was just not refreshed with his preaching. Perhaps the presence of God had left him. The blood of Jesus and the cross on which Jesus was sacrificed can never be replaced by anything. The wisdom of men, laced with scriptures, cannot replace the wisdom of the cross of Jesus Christ.

3. Joy comes to you through the presence of the Lord.

Thou wilt shew me the path of life: IN THY PRESENCE IS FULNESS OF JOY; at thy right hand there are pleasures for evermore.

Psalms 16:11

The presence of the Lord gives rise to joy. Inexplicable joy comes into the hearts of those who experience the presence of God. Today, people are taking anti-depressants when all they need is the presence of God. You will have joy, peace and happiness when you enjoy the presence of God. The atmosphere of depression, discouragement, disillusionment, discontentment are not possible in the presence of God. In the presence of God, there is joy!

4. **Direction for your life comes from the presence of the Lord.**

> Hear the right, O Lord, attend unto my cry, give ear unto my prayer, that goeth not out of feigned lips. LET MY SENTENCE COME FORTH FROM THY PRESENCE; let thine eyes behold the things that are equal.
>
> Psalms 17:1-2

The psalmist writes, "Let my sentence come from thy presence." Direction for your life comes from the presence of God. People who are in the presence of God rarely lack direction. When you are in the presence of a great person, you hear many things, you get to know the person's opinion and ideas about many things. It is because you are not in the presence of God that you lack His direction for your life. If you care to spend some more time in the presence of God, the sentence for your life will come forth speedily.

5. **You have good thoughts in the presence of God.**

> We have thought of thy LOVINGKINDNESS, O God, IN THE MIDST OF THY TEMPLE.
>
> Psalms 48:9

When you are in the midst of His temple, you think of God's loving kindness and goodness.

It is the mighty presence of God that causes you to experience thoughts of God's loving kindness. When you are away from the presence of God, you can be overwhelmed with evil thoughts. When you are away from the presence of God, you may even think that God is angry with you when, in fact, He is in love with you. God has good thoughts towards you but it is His presence that allows His goodness to fill your heart.

6. **Your enemy is destroyed by the presence of God.**

> I will be glad and rejoice in thee: I will sing praise to thy name, O thou most High. WHEN MINE ENEMIES ARE TURNED BACK, THEY SHALL FALL AND PERISH AT THY PRESENCE. For thou hast maintained my right and my cause; thou satest in the throne judging right.
> Psalms 9:2-4

> LET GOD ARISE, LET HIS ENEMIES BE SCATTERED: let them also that hate him flee before him. As smoke is driven away, so drive them away: as wax melteth before the fire, so let the wicked perish at the presence of God.
> Psalms 68:1-2

When your enemy prevails over you, it may be because you lack the presence of God in your life and ministry. By seeking the Lord and doing His will, you will cause a manifestation of God's presence in your life. This presence of God in your life will wipe out your enemies. It is the mighty presence of God that takes away evil from your life forever. "The Lord thy God in the midst of thee" is the presence of God. Notice this beautiful scripture in the book of Zephaniah. Indeed, the Lord God in your midst is your great blessing because evil is taken away.

> The Lord hath taken away thy judgments, he hath cast out thine enemy:
> the king of Israel, even THE LORD, IS IN THE MIDST OF THEE: THOU SHALT NOT SEE EVIL ANY More.
> Zephaniah 3:15

7. **The mighty presence of God causes salvation and the gathering of souls.**

> THE LORD THY GOD IN THE MIDST OF THEE IS MIGHTY; HE WILL SAVE, he will rejoice over thee with joy; he will rest in his love, he will joy over thee with singing. I WILL GATHER THEM that are sorrowful

for the solemn assembly, who are of thee, to whom the reproach of it was a burden.

Zephaniah 3:17-18

When the presence of God is departed there is no more salvation. Instead of salvation, there is business, profit making and a host of other distractions that take the ministry away from pure salvation and the gathering of souls for the kingdom of God.

The Lord God in the midst of us is the One who saves. When the Lord God is no longer in our midst then there is no more salvation. When the presence of God is no longer there, all testimonies have to do with money, business and profit-making.

The Lord thy God in the midst of thee will save people. Indeed, it is also true that God's power in your midst can save you from poverty and difficulty. The Lord God in the midst of thee will gather people and this will lead to church growth. It is the presence of God that leads to mega churches. Notice how the scripture in Zephaniah teaches that the Lord in our midst will gather people from everywhere to worship the Lord.

8. The mighty presence of God causes many nations to be added to the Lord.

Sing and rejoice, O daughter of Zion: for, lo, I come, and I WILL DWELL IN THE MIDST OF THEE, SAITH THE LORD. AND MANY NATIONS SHALL BE JOINED TO THE LORD in that day, and shall be my people: and I will dwell in the midst of thee, and thou shalt know that the Lord of hosts hath sent me unto thee.

And the Lord shall inherit Judah his portion in the holy land, and shall choose Jerusalem again. Be silent, O all flesh, before the Lord: for he is raised up out of his holy habitation.

Zechariah 2:10-13

The prophecy is clear: I will dwell in the midst of thee and many nations will be joined to the Lord. The presence of God truly brings about a worldwide and international ministry of soul winning and church planting.

The presence of God gives you an international ministry. The failure of the church to win the nations is a sign that the presence of God has departed from the church.

Today, most churches are no longer winning the nations to the Lord. Many years ago, the church in America, the church in Switzerland and the church in England reached out to the nations and spread the good news of Jesus Christ to the nations. Today, this is not happening. The presence of God seems to have departed. Looking inward and only seeking to build yourself up financially is not a sign of the presence of God.

The prophecy is clear: "I will dwell in the midst of thee and many nations will be joined to the Lord." The presence of God truly brings about a worldwide and international ministry of soul winning and church planting.

9. The mighty presence of God causes excellent things to be done.

And in that day thou shalt say, O Lord, I will praise thee: though thou wast angry with me, thine anger is turned away, and thou comfortedst me.

Behold, God is my salvation; I will trust, and not be afraid: for the Lord Jehovah is my strength and my song; he also is become my salvation. Therefore with joy shall ye draw water out of the wells of salvation.

And in that day shall ye say, PRAISE THE LORD, CALL UPON HIS NAME DECLARE HIS DOINGS AMONG THE PEOPLE make mention that his name is exalted.

Sing unto the Lord; for HE HATH DONE EXCELLENT THINGS: this is known in all the earth.

Cry out and shout, thou inhabitant of Zion: FOR GREAT IS THE HOLY ONE OF ISRAEL IN THE MIDST OF THEE.

                                                    Isaiah 12:1-6

God does strange and marvellous things in our lives when His presence is there. It is the presence of God that causes excellent, beautiful and wonderful things to happen. Seek to be obedient to the Lord and you will enjoy His presence. When you enjoy His presence, you will see excellent things being done all the time. The Holy One of Israel in the midst of thee is the cause of excellent things. When you see someone who is able to do excellent and wonderful things for God, it is because of the Lord in the midst of His people. I once saw a glorious church. It was beautiful to behold. It was excellent in its working. I knew immediately that the Lord was in the midst of that church.

10. The mighty presence of God causes you not to be astonished or powerless.

Why shouldest thou be as A MAN ASTONIED, as a mighty man THAT CANNOT SAVE? YET THOU, O LORD, ART IN THE MIDST OF US, and we are called by thy name; LEAVE US NOT.

Jeremiah 14:9

Through the presence of God you will never be surprised and astonished. If you enjoy the mighty power of God, you will notice how demons flee from you. When the presence of God is on your life, nothing can surprise you. You will be calm because you know that the Lord is with you.

Chapter 19

Divine Signs of the Presence of God in Your Ministry

And he said unto him, If thy presence go not with me, carry us not up hence. FOR WHEREIN SHALL IT BE KNOWN HERE THAT I AND THY PEOPLE HAVE FOUND GRACE IN THY SIGHT? IS IT NOT IN THAT THOU GOEST WITH US?...

Exodus 33:15-16

1. **DIVINE FEARLESSNESS:** Your ministry is guaranteed fearlessness, deliverance, victory and success by the divine presence.

   BE NOT AFRAID of their faces: FOR I AM WITH THEE to deliver thee, saith the Lord.

   Jeremiah 1:8

2. **DIVINE SURVIVAL:** Your ministry is guaranteed supernatural survival because of the presence of God.

   For, behold, I have made thee this day a defenced city, and an iron pillar, and brasen walls against the whole land, against the kings of Judah, against the princes thereof, against the priests thereof, and against the people of the land. And THEY SHALL FIGHT AGAINST THEE; BUT THEY SHALL NOT PREVAIL AGAINST THEE; for I AM WITH THEE, SAITH THE LORD, TO DELIVER THEE.

   Jeremiah 1:18-19

3. **DIVINE IMPENETRABILITY:** Your ministry is guaranteed divine impenetrability: You are airtight, long lasting - because of the presence of God.

   And I will make thee unto this people a fenced brasen wall: and they shall fight against thee, but THEY SHALL NOT PREVAIL AGAINST THEE: FOR I AM WITH THEE TO SAVE THEE AND TO DELIVER THEE, SAITH THE LORD. And I will deliver thee out of the hand of the wicked, and I will redeem thee out of the hand of the terrible.

   Jeremiah 15:20-21

4. **DIVINE FRUITFULNESS:** Your ministry is guaranteed divine fruitfulness because of the presence of God. **Many people! Many nations! Many conversions! Much following** - Because of the presence of God!

Thus saith the Lord of hosts; It shall yet come to pass, that there shall come people, and the inhabitants of many cities: And the inhabitants of one city shall go to another, saying, Let us go speedily to pray before the Lord and to seek the Lord of hosts: I will go also. Yea, many people and strong nations shall come to seek the Lord of hosts in Jerusalem, and to pray before the Lord. Thus saith the Lord of hosts; In those days it shall come to pass, that TEN MEN SHALL TAKE HOLD OUT OF ALL LANGUAGES OF THE NATIONS, EVEN SHALL TAKE HOLD OF THE SKIRT OF HIM THAT IS A JEW, SAYING, WE WILL GO WITH YOU: FOR WE HAVE HEARD THAT GOD IS WITH YOU.

Zechariah 8:20-23

5. **DIVINE APPROVAL: Your ministry is guaranteed divine approval because of the presence of God.**

And he said unto him, IF THY PRESENCE GO NOT WITH ME, CARRY US NOT UP HENCE. FOR WHEREIN SHALL IT BE KNOWN HERE THAT I AND THY PEOPLE HAVE FOUND GRACE IN THY SIGHT? Is it not in that thou goest with us? So shall we be separated, I and thy people, from all the people that are upon the face of the earth.

Exodus 33:15-16

6. **DIVINE FAVOUR: Your ministry is given great favour because of the presence of God.**

And the angel came in unto her, and said, Hail, THOU THAT ART HIGHLY FAVOURED, THE LORD IS WITH THEE: blessed art thou among women. And when she saw him, she was troubled at his saying, and cast in her mind what manner of salutation this should be.

Luke 1:28-29

7. **DIVINE MAGNIFICATION: Your ministry will be magnified because of the presence of God.**

And the Lord said unto Joshua, THIS DAY WILL I BEGIN TO MAGNIFY THEE in the sight of all Israel, that they may know that, as I was with Moses, SO I WILL BE WITH THEE.

Joshua 3:7

8. **DIVINE BOLDNESS: Your ministry is guaranteed boldness, courage, fearless expansion and advancement because of the presence of God.**

This book of the law shall not depart out of thy mouth; but thou shalt meditate therein day and night, that thou mayest observe to do according to all that is written therein: for then thou shalt make thy way prosperous, and then thou shalt have good success. Have not I commanded thee? BE STRONG AND OF A GOOD COURAGE; BE NOT AFRAID, NEITHER BE THOU DISMAYED: FOR THE LORD THY GOD IS WITH THEE whithersoever thou goest.

Joshua 1:8-9

9. **DIVINE GUARANTEES: Your ministry is commissioned and guaranteed by the presence of God.**

And Moses went and spake these words unto all Israel. And he said unto them, I am an hundred and twenty years old this day; I can no more go out and come in: also the Lord hath said unto me, Thou shalt not go over this Jordan. The Lord thy God, he will go over before thee, and he will destroy these nations from before thee, and thou shalt possess them: and Joshua, he shall go over before thee, as the Lord hath said.

And the Lord shall do unto them as he did to Sihon and to Og, kings of the Amorites, and unto the land of them, whom he destroyed. And the Lord shall give them up before your face, that ye may do unto them according unto all the commandments which I have commanded you.

Be strong and of a good courage, fear not, nor be afraid of them: for the Lord thy God, he it is that doth go with thee; he will not fail thee, nor forsake thee.

And Moses called unto Joshua, and said unto him in the sight of all Israel, Be strong and of a good courage: for thou must go with this people unto the land which the Lord hath sworn unto their fathers to give them; and thou shalt cause them to inherit it. And THE LORD, HE IT IS THAT DOTH GO BEFORE THEE; HE WILL BE WITH THEE, HE WILL NOT FAIL THEE, neither forsake thee: fear not, neither be dismayed.

Deuteronomy 31:1-8

10. **ENDLESS DIVINE VICTORIES: Your ministry is guaranteed victory in every battle not because you are always right or because you are clever but because of the presence of God.**

WHEN THOU GOEST OUT TO BATTLE against thine enemies, and seest horses, and chariots, and a people more than thou, BE NOT AFRAID OF THEM: FOR THE LORD THY GOD IS WITH THEE, which brought thee up out of the land of Egypt.

Deuteronomy 20:1

11. **DIVINE JUDGMENT ON THOSE WHO PERSECUTE YOU: Every ministry will have persecutors. The presence of God guarantees five disasters for those who fight against you.**

But THE LORD IS WITH ME as a mighty terrible one: therefore my persecutors shall stumble, and they shall not prevail: they shall be greatly ashamed; for they shall not prosper: their everlasting confusion shall never be forgotten.

Jeremiah 20:11

1. They will stumble because God's presence is with you!
2. They will not prevail against you because God's presence is with you!
3. They will be ashamed because God's presence is with you!
4. They will not prosper because God's presence is with you!
5. They will be confused because God's presence is with you!

Chapter 20

Moments in the Presence of God

Cast me not away from thy presence; and take not thy holy spirit from me.

Psalms 51:11

When God calls you, you can expect His presence to be manifest. The presence of God was revealed throughout the ministry of Moses. From his call through different events that happened in his life, we see the presence of God being manifested beautifully. As you read this chapter, I want you to expect the presence of God to be manifest in your ministry. Like Jacob said, "The Lord was in this place and I knew it not." It is possible to experience the presence of God and not even know that you are experiencing it. Through this chapter, I want you to recognize moments of His presence. You will begin to see the evidence that the presence of God is with you in your ministry.

1. Expect the presence of God when you are called.

> And the angel of the Lord appeared unto him in a flame of fire out of the midst of a bush: and he looked, and, behold, the bush burned with fire, and the bush was not consumed. And Moses said, I will now turn aside, and see this great sight, why the bush is not burnt. And WHEN THE LORD SAW THAT HE TURNED ASIDE TO SEE, GOD CALLED UNTO HIM OUT OF THE MIDST OF THE BUSH, and said, Moses, Moses. And he said, Here am I. And he said, draw not nigh hither: put off thy shoes from off thy feet, for the place whereon thou standest is holy ground. Moreover HE SAID, I AM THE GOD OF THY FATHER, the God of Abraham, the God of Isaac, and the God of Jacob. And Moses hid his face; for he was afraid to look upon God.
>
> Exodus 3:2-6

I can understand why you would think to yourself that Moses' experiences have nothing to do with you. However, the Bible teaches that the things that have happened are examples that we should learn from. Moses' experience of the presence of God during his call to ministry is similar to what you will experience when God calls you.

There may be no burning bush but the voice of God will be clear and God will have your attention because of His presence.

Most of the time, when God calls you, the presence of God is around you. In that moment there is a wonderful presence that descends on you. When you are anointed, the Spirit of God is upon you. But when you are being called the Spirit of God is with you. His presence causes you to see and to notice certain things. The presence of God descended into the life of Moses, causing a bush to burn. The burning bush was the sign of God's presence. As God's presence was manifested, a voice came and he had his famous interaction with God.

There are times I feel His presence when I read my Bible. The Spirit of revelation and truth flow in me and I am able to see great things out of His word. Many years ago, God called me to serve Him. That morning the presence of God was strong. And as I read the scripture, "Give thyself wholly to these things..." I felt God was speaking and that I had to give up everything else in the world. A great ministry was born from that interaction on that fateful morning. Many people are surrounded by the presence of God when they hear a call to ministry.

2. Expect the presence of God when you are travelling.

And they took their journey from Succoth, and encamped in Etham, in the edge of the wilderness. And THE LORD WENT BEFORE THEM BY DAY IN A PILLAR OF A CLOUD, to lead them the way; and by night in a pillar of fire, to give them light; to go by day and night: He took not away the pillar of the cloud by day, nor the pillar of fire by night, from before the people.

Exodus 13:20-22

The presence of God goes with you as you are on the move. You can expect the presence of God to give you guidance. There are many people in ministry who are no longer led by the Holy Spirit. The children of Israel never disconnected themselves from the pillar of cloud or the pillar of fire. That was what kept them alive. In the same way, you cannot disconnect from the presence of God if you are being led by the Spirit. The presence of God is a wonderful guiding post for ministry.

3. Expect the presence of God when you need protection.

> And the angel of God, which went before the camp of Israel, removed and went behind them; and THE PILLAR OF THE CLOUD WENT FROM BEFORE THEIR FACE, AND STOOD BEHIND THEM: And it came BETWEEN THE CAMP OF THE EGYPTIANS AND THE CAMP OF ISRAEL; AND IT WAS A CLOUD AND DARKNESS TO THEM, but it gave light by night to these: SO THAT THE ONE CAME NOT NEAR THE OTHER ALL THE NIGHT.
>
> Exodus 14:19-20

The presence of God served as a protection for Moses and the children of Israel. The pillar of cloud by day and the pillar of fire by night prevented the demonic hordes of Egypt from coming close. Today, the demonic hordes that seek to destroy you are prevented from coming close because of the presence of God.

When the presence of God is with you, you will have divine protection. It may not be a pillar of cloud or a pillar of fire but God will definitely protect you. The presence of God is a protection against many evils. Certain things that would have happened to you did not happen just because of the presence of God.

4. Expect the presence of God when you are in trouble.

> And the Egyptians pursued, and went in after them to the midst of the sea, even all Pharaoh's horses, his chariots, and his horsemen. And it came to pass, that IN THE MORNING WATCH THE LORD LOOKED UNTO THE HOST OF THE EGYPTIANS THROUGH THE PILLAR OF FIRE AND OF THE CLOUD, AND TROUBLED THE HOST OF THE EGYPTIANS, and took off their chariot wheels, that they drave them heavily: so that the

Egyptians said, Let us flee from the face of Israel; for the Lord fighteth for them against the Egyptians.

Exodus 14:23-25

Your enemies will be troubled because God is with you. The power of God that broods around you will cause trouble to your enemies. People will start dying as they attack you, as they intimidate you, as they plan against you and as they seek to embarrass you.

5.   Expect the presence of God when you pray.

> And Moses took the tabernacle, and pitched it without the camp, afar off from the camp, and called it the Tabernacle of the congregation. And it came to pass, that every one which sought the Lord went out unto the tabernacle of the congregation, which was without the camp. And it came to pass, when Moses went out unto the tabernacle, that all the people rose up, and stood every man at his tent door, and looked after Moses, until he was gone into the tabernacle.
>
> And it came to pass, AS MOSES ENTERED INTO THE TABERNACLE, THE CLOUDY PILLAR DESCENDED, AND STOOD AT THE DOOR OF THE TABERNACLE, AND THE LORD TALKED WITH MOSES. And all the people saw the cloudy pillar stand at the tabernacle door: and all the people rose up and worshipped, every man in his tent door.
>
> And the Lord spake unto Moses face to face, as a man speaketh unto his friend. And he turned again into the camp: but his servant Joshua, the son of Nun, a young man, departed not out of the tabernacle.

Exodus 33:7-11

Just as the pillar descended over the tent of Moses when he went into prayer, the presence of God descends around you when you go into prayer. There is always an aura of the presence of God with those who spend time in prayer. God is with them and His presence is with them. From today, as you seek the Lord in prayer, you will experience and enjoy more of His presence in your life.

6. Expect the presence of God when you seek God.

And he said, My presence shall go with thee, and I will give thee rest. And he said unto him, If thy presence go not with me, carry us not up hence. For wherein shall it be known here that I and thy people have found grace in thy sight? Is it not in that thou goest with us? So shall we be separated, I and thy people, from all the people that are upon the face of the earth. And the Lord said unto Moses, I will do this thing also that thou hast spoken: for thou hast found grace in my sight, and I know thee by name. And he said, I beseech thee, shew me thy glory and he said, I will make all my goodness pass before thee, and I will proclaim the name of the Lord before thee; and will be gracious to whom I will be gracious, and will shew mercy on whom I will shew mercy. And he said, Thou canst not see my face: for there shall no man see me, and live.

Exodus 33:14-20

God's presence appeared in Moses' life when he sought the Lord. Moses asked for the presence of God and he got it! The presence of God indeed brings the goodness of God into your life. Expect God to be gracious to you when you seek Him.

7. Expect the presence of God to bring about judgment.

Miriam and Aaron began to talk against Moses because of his Cushite wife, for he had married a Cushite. . . (Now Moses was a very humble man, more humble than anyone else on the face of the earth.)

At once the Lord said to Moses, Aaron and Miriam, "Come out to the tent of meeting, all three of you." So the three of them went out. Then the Lord came down in a pillar of cloud; he stood at the entrance to the tent and summoned Aaron and Miriam. When the two of them stepped forward. . .

But this is not true of my servant Moses; he is faithful in all my house. With him I speak face to face, clearly and not in riddles; he sees the form of the Lord. Why then were you not afraid to speak against my servant Moses?" THE ANGER OF THE LORD BURNED AGAINST THEM, AND HE LEFT THEM. WHEN THE CLOUD LIFTED FROM ABOVE THE TENT, MIRIAM'S SKIN WAS LEPROUS - it became as white as snow. Aaron turned toward her and saw that she had a defiling skin disease,

Numbers 12:1, 3-5,7-10 (NIV)

The presence of God brought judgment to Miriam and Aaron. Miriam was struck with leprosy and death because they had spoken against Moses. When the presence of God appeared, they were struck with a fatal disease. Watch out for people who carry the presence of God around! Misbehaving in their presence may lead to judgment and your death.

8.   Expect the presence of God to tell about the future.

And the Lord said unto Moses, Behold, thy days approach that thou must die: call Joshua, and present yourselves in the tabernacle of the congregation, that I may give him a charge. And Moses and Joshua went, and presented themselves in the tabernacle of the congregation.

And THE LORD APPEARED IN THE TABERNACLE IN A PILLAR OF A CLOUD: and the pillar of the cloud stood over the door of the tabernacle. AND THE LORD SAID UNTO MOSES, BEHOLD, THOU SHALT SLEEP WITH THY FATHERS; AND THIS PEOPLE WILL RISE UP, AND GO A WHORING AFTER THE GODS OF THE STRANGERS OF THE LAND, whither they go to be among them, and will forsake me, and break my covenant which I have made with them.

Deuteronomy 31:14-16

Once again, the presence of God led to blessings for the ministry of Moses. A clear prophecy of the future was given to Moses when the presence of God manifested. The prophecy was unbelievable. It was about how these children of Israel who had seen the goodness of God would behave in the future.

Who would ever have thought that God's people who had seen His power and miracles would one day turn against Him? Today, many Israelites are atheists. God's special people no longer believe in Him, in spite of all that He has done for them. Through the manifestation of the presence of God, you will be shown the future.

Chapter 21

Strange Happenings in the Presence of God

And THE LORD WENT BEFORE THEM BY DAY IN A PILLAR OF A CLOUD, to lead them the way; and BY NIGHT IN A PILLAR OF FIRE, to give them light; to go by day and night:

Exodus 13:21

The ark of God was a physical manifestation of God's presence. There was a time in which God's presence was strongly manifested through the ark. Wherever the ark was, God was there. Wherever the presence of God is, there are manifestations. There will be a wide variety of manifestations of the presence of God in your life and ministry from now onwards.

1. Death to all the mockers of God's presence.

And the Philistines took the ark of God, and brought it from Eben-ezer unto Ashdod. WHEN THE PHILISTINES TOOK THE ARK OF GOD, they brought it into the house of Dagon, and set it by Dagon.

And when they of Ashdod arose early on the morrow, behold, Dagon was fallen upon his face to the earth before the ark of the Lord. And they took Dagon, and set him in his place again. And when they arose early on the morrow morning, behold, Dagon was fallen upon his face to the ground before the ark of the Lord ; and the head of Dagon and both the palms of his hands were cut off upon the threshold; only the stump of Dagon was left to him. Therefore neither the priests of Dagon, nor any that come into Dagon's house, tread on the threshold of Dagon in Ashdod unto this day.

But THE HAND OF THE LORD WAS HEAVY UPON THEM OF ASHDOD, AND HE DESTROYED THEM, AND SMOTE THEM WITH EMERODS, even Ashdod and the coasts thereof. And when the men of Ashdod saw that it was so, they said, The ark of the God of Israel shall not abide with us: for his hand is sore upon us, and upon Dagon our god. . .

So they sent and gathered together all the lords of the Philistines, and said, Send away the ark of the God of Israel, and let it go again to his own place, that it slay us not, and our people: for THERE WAS A DEADLY DESTRUCTION THROUGHOUT ALL THE CITY; the hand of God was very heavy there. And the men that died not were smitten with the emerods: and the cry of the city went up to heaven.

1 Samuel 5:1-7, 11-12

The presence of God, in the form of the Ark of the Covenant, caused death to the enemies of God. Over and over, we see that the presence of God in a minister's life brings judgment to those who mock God's servants. The Philistines discovered this firsthand. They carried the ark of God into their camp and were plagued with diseases and death. They recognized that they had toyed with the presence of God and were paying dearly for it.

Not every man of God carries the presence of God in a certain way. However, some of God's servants do carry the presence of God with them. It is important not to toy with such servants of God. You can be struck with diseases and death because you took the presence of God for granted. You must be quick to recognize those who carry a strong presence of God and avoid making mistakes in relation to them. A mistake could cost you dearly.

2. Judgment to all the mockers of God's presence.

Again, David gathered together all the chosen men of Israel, thirty thousand. And David arose, and went with all the people that were with him from Baale of Judah, to bring up from thence the ark of God, whose name is called by the name of the Lord of hosts that dwelleth between the cherubims. And they set the ark of God upon a new cart, and brought it out of the house of Abinadab that was in Gibeah: and Uzzah and Ahio, the sons of Abinadab, drave the new cart.

And they brought it out of the house of Abinadab which was at Gibeah, accompanying the ark of God: and Ahio went before the ark. And David and all the house of Israel played before the Lord on all manner of instruments made of fir wood, even on harps, and on psalteries, and on timbrels, and on cornets, and on cymbals.

And when they came to Nachon's threshingfloor, UZZAH PUT FORTH HIS HAND TO THE ARK OF GOD, AND TOOK HOLD OF IT; FOR THE OXEN SHOOK IT. AND THE ANGER OF THE LORD WAS KINDLED AGAINST UZZAH; AND GOD SMOTE HIM THERE FOR HIS ERROR; and there he died by the ark of God. And DAVID WAS DISPLEASED, BECAUSE THE LORD HAD MADE A BREACH UPON UZZAH: and he called the name of the place Perez-uzzah to this day. AND DAVID WAS AFRAID OF THE LORD THAT DAY, AND SAID, HOW SHALL THE ARK OF THE LORD COME TO ME?

2 Samuel 6:1-9

It is important to know how to relate in the presence of God. Familiarity with God's servants and the presence of God can be costly. Whenever a man of God seems easily available, you must not allow that to deceive you. The strong presence of God around their lives and ministry may mean more than you care to acknowledge.

The ark of God seemed to be a common thing in those days and Uzzah simply stretched out his hand to balance the ark nicely. Unfortunately, that displeased the Lord and he died for his mistake of being too casual. Beware of casual prophets! Few people are able to handle casual men of God. You may stretch out your hand to correct them but die for your mistake.

There are men of God who do not use big words. Neither do they wear royal clothing to give an aura of specialness and mystery. However, they may be covered with a strong presence of God. Stretching out your hand to correct them or to bring balance may cost you your life.

There are wives who have died because they thought to bring balance into their husband's ministry. "I want to balance your messages," they may say. "I want to bring a balance to the things you do." "You are out of balance and out of order," they think.

This was Uzzah's mistake. He sought to bring balance to the presence of God. God's presence is never out of balance. No human being can correct God. No human being can rebuke God. Watch out for those who feel they can correct God's servants.

Some people peeped into the ark of God. Once again, the ark of God looked very accessible, very normal and very ordinary. It is these apparently harmless characteristics that make people trivialize the presence of God. People think they are dealing with a mere man. But they find out that they are dealing with God. When Jesus came to this world they treated Him very badly. Instead of crowning Him with praise, they crowned Him with thorns. Instead of honouring Him they mocked at Him. But they paid dearly for their failure to recognize the presence of God in their midst.

The entire city of Jerusalem was wiped out after Jesus died on the cross. Be careful when you treat God's servant as though you are dealing with the devil. Jesus was dealt with as a criminal and an evil man. Even Barabbas was considered to be of more value than Jesus. Jesus was crucified between thieves, implying that He was a thief. For all these things, the Jews have never ceased to pay the price of not recognizing God's presence.

When the ark of God came into the field of Joshua the Beth-shemite, they equally made a mistake in handling the presence of God. They peeped into the ark and over fifty thousand people died. Indeed, God's presence must not be trifled with. Be careful of men who carry a strong presence of God. They often cause death to those who mock them.

> And the cart came into the field of Joshua, a Beth-shemite, and stood there, where there was a great stone: and they clave the wood of the cart, and offered the kine a burnt offering unto the Lord. And the Levites took down the ark of the Lord, and the coffer that was with it, wherein the jewels of gold were, and put them on the great stone: and the men of Beth-shemesh offered burnt offerings and sacrificed sacrifices the same day unto the Lord . . .

And HE SMOTE THE MEN OF BETH-SHEMESH, BECAUSE THEY HAD LOOKED INTO THE ARK OF THE LORD, even he smote of the people FIFTY THOUSAND AND THREESCORE AND TEN MEN: and the people lamented, because the Lord had smitten many of the people with a great slaughter.

And THE MEN OF BETH-SHEMESH SAID, WHO IS ABLE TO STAND BEFORE THIS HOLY LORD GOD? And to whom shall he go up from us? And they sent messengers to the inhabitants of Kirjath-jearim, saying, The Philistines have brought again the ark of the Lord ; come ye down, and fetch it up to you.

1 Samuel 6:14-15,19-21

3. Prosperity to all the lovers of God's presence.

So David would not remove the ark of the Lord unto him into the city of David: but David carried it aside into the house of Obededom the Gittite. And THE ARK OF THE LORD CONTINUED IN THE HOUSE OF OBEDEDOM THE GITTITE THREE MONTHS: AND THE LORD BLESSED OBEDEDOM, AND ALL HIS HOUSEHOLD.

And it was told king David, saying, The Lord hath blessed the house of Obededom, and all that pertaineth unto him, because of the ark of God. So David went and brought up the ark of God from the house of Obededom into the city of David with gladness.

2 Samuel 6:10-12

Prosperity came to Obededom's household because the ark of God was there. The presence of God enveloped the household of Obededom. Instead of death, there was prosperity. The presence of God can go far right or far left. Things will work out just because the presence of God is there. Money will be given to you just because of the presence of God.

Many people work very hard but never really prosper. Why is this? The ground has been cursed to yield thorns and thistles.

Man's life is cursed to yield a little bread with much sweat. Satan is overseeing these curses and ensuring that poverty and financial difficulty are the order of the day. The presence of God is the power of God that overshadows your household and suspends the curse.

Through the presence of God, the curse is suspended and prosperity and abundance are released. Few people in this world have much to show for all their hard work. Most of us just have sweat to show for our years of living on this earth. We have eaten bread, we have had something to drink and we have sweated a lot. This is man without the presence of God. When Obededom experienced the presence of God, the curse was broken and his story was changed. This is what will happen to you when the presence of God is manifested in your life.

4. Calmness to all who respect God's presence.

> And the men of Kirjath-jearim came, and fetched up the ark of the Lord, and brought it into the house of Abinadab in the hill, and sanctified Eleazar his son to keep the ark of the Lord. And IT CAME TO PASS, WHILE THE ARK ABODE IN KIRJATH-JEARIM, THAT THE TIME WAS LONG; FOR IT WAS TWENTY YEARS: and all the house of Israel lamented after the Lord.
>
> 1 Samuel 7:1-2

The presence of God in the house of Abinadab was uneventful. This is the mystery of His presence. In His presence, there may be no physical action or reaction. It is this mysterious silence from God's presence that deceives human beings into thinking that there is no God. When Jesus died on the cross, there seemed to be no response from heaven. God allowed men to do whatever they wanted to the Son of God.

As the wickedness of men was revealed, God was silent and watched on as human beings played out the very worst of themselves. By the time Jesus died on the cross, the worst characteristics of humankind had been played out. There was no more denying that man was evil. There were no more excuses as to the wretchedness of human beings.

If anyone had asked the Pharisees whether they would crucify a prophet, they would have said, "Not at all!" But when a great prophet did come, all they did was to crucify Him.

Why was there no reaction from heaven? It was for the same reason that the stay of the ark of God in the house of Abinadab was uneventful.

Chapter 22

Reactions to God's Presence

The earth shook, the heavens also dropped at the presence of God: even Sinai itself was moved at the presence of God, the God of Israel.

Psalms 68:8

All through history there have been physical reactions to the presence of God. The Bible records many of these reactions. Both the Old Testament and the New Testament have records of how physical things react to the presence of God. Let us go through some of these amazing responses to the presence of God.

> And they came over unto the other side of the sea, into the country of the Gadarenes. And when he was come out of the ship, immediately there met him out of the tombs a man with an unclean spirit,
>
> Mark 5:1-2

Jesus' presence in the country of the Gadarenes caused amazing reactions in the spirit. Six thousand demons were transferred in response to the presence of Jesus. Please note that Jesus Christ did not have the opportunity to preach in the country of the Gadarenes. He never entered a synagogue and never had the chance to speak. His presence alone in that country caused a major reaction in the spirit.

Indeed, someone who carries the presence of God does not even have to preach in your church to cause a change in the spirit realm. A minister who carries the presence of God can cause everlasting changes to take place in your life and in your church.

1. EARTH SHAKING:

> O God, when thou wentest forth before thy people, when thou didst march through the wilderness; Selah: THE EARTH SHOOK, THE HEAVENS ALSO DROPPED AT THE PRESENCE OF GOD: even SINAI ITSELF WAS MOVED at the presence of God, the God of Israel. Thou, O God, didst send a plentiful rain, whereby thou didst confirm thine inheritance, when it was weary.
>
> Psalms 68:7-9

This scripture shows us that shaking occurs at the presence of God. Mountains are moved and the heavens release their rain at the presence of God. Do not be surprised if people shake and drop at the presence of God. The very building in which you are may shake when the presence of God is manifested. It is possible that earthquakes are a response to the presence of God. When the disciples prayed, the very place where they had the meeting was shaken.

And when they had prayed, THE PLACE WAS SHAKEN WHERE THEY WERE ASSEMBLED TOGETHER; and they were all filled with the Holy Ghost, and they spake the word of God with boldness.

Acts 4:31

2. MEN SHAKING:

For in my jealousy and in the fire of my wrath have I spoken, Surely in that day there shall be a great shaking in the land of Israel;

So that the fishes of the sea, and the fowls of the heaven, and the beasts of the field, and all creeping things that creep upon the earth, and ALL THE MEN THAT ARE UPON THE FACE OF THE EARTH, SHALL SHAKE AT MY PRESENCE, and the mountains shall be thrown down, and the steep places shall fall, and EVERY WALL SHALL FALL to the ground.

Ezekiel 38:19-20

Men also shake at the presence of God. This is not unusual. It is wonderful to see manifestations, such as shaking, in God's presence. You must desire the presence of God so much that all these manifestations will become a daily part of your life. Do not accept the Word but deny the power of God. The power of God can make people shake. Even mountains can be thrown down and walls can fall down.

3. **SOFTENING:**

THE HILLS MELTED LIKE WAX AT THE PRESENCE OF THE LORD, at the presence of the Lord of the whole earth.

> Psalms 97:5

The presence of God causes hard elements to soften. People who are resistant and unchangeable will yield and soften when the presence of God is there. Even the hills melt like wax in the presence of God.

4. **TREMBLING:**

When Israel went out of Egypt, the house of Jacob from a people of strange language; Judah was his sanctuary, and Israel his dominion. The sea saw it, and fled: Jordan was driven back. The mountains skipped like rams, and the little hills like lambs. What ailed thee, O thou sea, that thou fleddest? Thou Jordan, that thou wast driven back?

Ye mountains, that ye skipped like rams; and ye little hills, like lambs? TREMBLE, THOU EARTH, AT THE PRESENCE OF THE LORD, AT THE PRESENCE OF THE GOD OF JACOB;

> Psalms 114:1-7

People tremble at the presence of God. The scripture shows that even mountains will tremble when God's power is present. I have seen people tremble in the presence of the Lord. Pray that God's presence will be manifested at your meetings so that you see these tremblings and shakings that are clear manifestations of the Lord's presence.

5. **FLOWING:**

OH THAT THOU WOULDEST REND THE HEAVENS, THAT THOU WOULDEST COME DOWN, THAT THE MOUNTAINS MIGHT FLOW DOWN AT THY PRESENCE, As when the melting fire burneth, the fire causeth the waters to boil, to make thy name known to thine adversaries, that the nations may tremble at thy presence! When thou didst terrible things which we looked not for, thou camest down, the mountains flowed down at thy presence.

Isaiah 64:1-3

People are yielded, accommodating and interested when the presence of God is there. The mountains, which we know to be unmoveable are ready to flow in the presence of God. Do not forget the famous scripture, "Thy people shall be willing in the day of thy power." (Psalms 110:3). Willingness, yieldedness, cheerfulness and even a good attitude are all manifestations of God's presence in your ministry. When you are surrounded by unwilling, unhappy and discontented people, it is a sign that the presence of God is not there. Even unmoveable mountains flow at His presence. May every unmoveable and unyielding person begin to flow happily with you at the presence of God!

6. BURNING:

The mountains quake at him, and the hills melt, and THE EARTH IS BURNED AT HIS PRESENCE, yea, the world, and all that dwell therein. Who can stand before his indignation?

And who can abide in the fierceness of his anger? His fury is poured out like fire, and the rocks are thrown down by him.

Nahum 1:5-6

In the New Testament, the presence of God was always manifested in the ministry of Jesus. Burning and fire are manifestations of God's presence. Diseases are burnt away at God's presence. People are ignited at the presence of God. The presence of God brings fire to lukewarm and backslidden people. Even mountains are ignited and catch fire at the presence of God. You must expect all these manifestations as you enjoy the presence of God in your ministry.

7. **FALLING AND ROLLING:**

He answereth him, and saith, O faithless generation, how long shall I be with you? how long shall I suffer you? bring him unto me.

And they brought him unto him: and WHEN HE SAW HIM, STRAIGHTWAY THE SPIRIT TARE HIM; AND HE FELL ON THE GROUND, AND WALLOWED FOAMING.

Mark 9:19-20

When the evil spirit in the boy saw Jesus, he reacted instantly to the presence of God. The young man fell to the ground and rolled, foaming at the mouth. This was an instant reaction to the presence of God. In the ministry of Jesus, there were many manifestations of God's presence. Jesus Christ Himself was a manifestation of the presence of God.

8. **FALLING DOWN:**

And WHEN I SAW HIM, I FELL AT HIS FEET AS DEAD. And he laid his right hand upon me, saying unto me, Fear not; I am the first and the last:

Revelation 1:17

When John the revelator saw Jesus, his reaction was to fall to the ground as though he was dead. The presence of God often causes people to fall down.

9. **INABILITY TO STAND:**

It came even to pass, as the trumpeters and singers were as one, to make one sound to be heard in praising and thanking the Lord; and when they lifted up their voice with the trumpets and cymbals and instruments of musick, and praised the Lord, saying, For he is good; for his mercy endureth for ever: that then the house was filled with a cloud, even the house of the Lord; so that THE PRIESTS COULD NOT STAND TO MINISTER BY REASON OF

THE CLOUD: FOR THE GLORY OF THE LORD HAD FILLED THE HOUSE OF GOD.

2 Chronicles 5:13-14

Entire congregations can fall at the presence of God. At the dedication of the temple, the power of God filled the temple and the presence was so strong that they were unable to stand. The priests could not stand! The people could not stand! This is a strong manifestation of the presence of God. As you seek the presence of God, you will experience all these in your ministry.

10. TRANSFIGURATION:

And after six days JESUS TAKETH PETER, JAMES, AND JOHN HIS BROTHER, AND BRINGETH THEM UP INTO AN HIGH MOUNTAIN APART, AND WAS TRANSFIGURED BEFORE THEM: and his face did shine as the sun, and his raiment was white as the light. And, behold, there appeared unto them Moses and Elias talking with him. Then answered Peter, and said unto Jesus, Lord, it is good for us to be here: if thou wilt, let us make here three tabernacles; one for thee, and one for Moses, and one for Elias. While he yet spake, behold, a bright cloud overshadowed them: and behold a voice out of the cloud, which said, This is my beloved Son, in whom I am well pleased; hear ye him. And when the disciples heard it, they fell on their face, and were sore afraid. And Jesus came and touched them, and said, Arise, and be not afraid. And when they had lifted up their eyes, they saw no man, save Jesus only.

Matthew 17:1-8

Jesus Christ was transfigured when the presence of God was manifested. Peter, James and John saw a different side of Jesus. When the presence of God is at work, you often see the man of God differently. The man of God will seem more supernatural and more powerful than a mere man. That is what the presence of God does!

Chapter 23

Experience the Continuous Presence of God

And THE LORD WENT BEFORE THEM BY DAY in a pillar of a cloud, to lead them the way; and BY NIGHT in a pillar of fire, to give them light; TO GO BY DAY AND NIGHT:

Exodus 13:21

The presence of God is something that seemed to come and go. Indeed, the people who experienced the presence of God did not seem to experience His presence continuously, but intermittently. However, some people seemed to have experienced God's presence continuously. One of the people who walked with God and therefore experienced God's presence continuously was Enoch.

Enoch and the Continuous Presence

> And Enoch WALKED WITH GOD after he begat Methuselah three hundred years, and begat sons and daughters: And all the days of Enoch were three hundred sixty and five years: And Enoch WALKED WITH GOD: and he was not; for god took him.
>
> Genesis 5:22-24

To continually dwell in the presence of God is not easy. Most of us experience the presence of God intermittently. The reward for staying continually in the presence of God was that Enoch transitioned from this life into the next without seeing death. To be absent from the body is to be present with the Lord. As soon as a believer dies, he is instantly present with the Lord.

If the presence of God is continuous on your life, dying will not be difficult. It will be a transition from one level of the presence of God to another. If, for instance, a Korean travels to an African country and lives amongst Koreans, eats Korean food, visits Korean restaurants and has only Korean friends, travelling back to Korea will not be such a drastic experience because even in Africa, he virtually lived in the presence of Koreans.

This is what it is like to transition from the presence of God on earth to the presence of God in heaven. As you walk in the presence of God on earth, you experience heavenly things continuously whilst on earth. Indeed, you are experiencing heaven on earth. To go to heaven will be the smallest transition ever.

Noah and the Continuous Presence

These are the generations of Noah: Noah was a just man and perfect in his generations, and NOAH WALKED WITH GOD. And Noah begat three sons, Shem, Ham, and Japheth. The earth also was corrupt before God, and the earth was filled with violence. And God looked upon the earth, and, behold, it was corrupt; for all flesh had corrupted his way upon the earth. AND GOD SAID UNTO NOAH, The end of all flesh is come before me; for the earth is filled with violence through them; and, behold, I will destroy them with the earth. MAKE THEE AN ARK OF GOPHER WOOD; rooms shalt thou make in the ark, and shalt pitch it within and without with pitch.

Genesis 6:9-14

Noah walked in the continuous presence of God. As Noah walked in the continuous presence of God, God chose him for a momentous and historic job. God gave him the privilege of becoming the second founder of the human race after God wiped out the entire human race. As the human race deteriorated, God decided to wipe out all the descendants of Adam and restart the human race. He could find only one person good enough for this awesome responsibility. It was someone who had walked closely and continuously with Him.

Today, if you walk in the presence of God, God will choose you to do great things. Perhaps you are jealous about how God is using certain people but not using you. You may think He is using them because they are Americans or Koreans. But it may be none of the reasons that you think. Continually walking in the presence of God gives such favour and causes amazing things to happen. Both Enoch and Noah experienced the unimaginable because they dwelt continually in God's presence.

Could it be that some of us experience the presence of God so infrequently that we are missing out on God's best for us? How many minutes every week do you experience the presence of God?

You and the Continuous Presence

If we live in the Spirit, let us also walk in the Spirit.

Galatians 5:25

You can walk in the continuous presence of God. It is possible! You can live in the Spirit and you can walk in the Spirit. The more you walk in the Spirit, the more you live in the Spirit! If you walk in something long enough you end up living in it. Begin to operate and live mostly in the Spirit! The more you walk in the presence of God, the less you fulfil the lusts of the flesh.

This I say then, Walk in the Spirit, and ye shall not fulfil the lust of the flesh.

Galatians 5:16

Chapter 24

His Presence is a Prophecy

> **Again the word of the Lord of hosts came to me, saying, THUS SAITH THE LORD of hosts; ... I AM RETURNED UNTO ZION, AND WILL DWELL IN THE MIDST OF JERUSALEM: ...**
>
> **Zechariah 8:1, 3**

I bless you with this prophecy of the presence of God. You shall experience the presence of God in your life.

Indeed, there is a great prophecy of how the Lord will dwell in the presence of His people. This prophecy must be a great source of encouragement to you and to me. Today, Israel is waiting for the arrival of the Messiah who will dwell physically with them in Jerusalem. But we know that He has come already. He is already in our midst. He said, "The Spirit of truth; whom the world cannot receive, because it seeth him not, neither knoweth him: but ye know him; for he dwelleth with you, and shall be in you." (John 14:17).

He is already with us. He has come into our midst and the prophecy of His presence is being fulfilled today.

His presence will bring about all the changes we hope for and His presence will lead to all the blessings we desire. Let us look at the prophecy of how the presence of God will transform everything.

1. **The prophecy of the coming presence. The prophecy of God dwelling in our midst.**

   Again the word of the Lord of hosts came to me, saying, Thus saith the Lord of hosts; I was jealous for Zion with great jealousy, and I was jealous for her with great fury.

   Thus saith the Lord; I AM RETURNED UNTO ZION, AND WILL DWELL IN THE MIDST OF JERUSALEM: and Jerusalem shall be called a city of truth; and the mountain of the Lord of hosts the holy mountain.

   Zechariah 8:1-3

2. **There will be long life and many men who will survive to old age. God promises to dwell in the midst of Jerusalem.** Because of His presence in Jerusalem, people will live long. Old men and old women will walk in the streets.

Thus saith the Lord of hosts; THERE SHALL YET OLD MEN AND OLD WOMEN DWELL IN THE STREETS OF JERUSALEM, and every man with his staff in his hand for very age.

Zechariah 8:4

3. **There will be happy children playing around. God has promised to dwell in the midst of Jerusalem and in the midst of Zion.** *His presence will cause the blessing of boys and girls playing in the streets. Through the presence of God in your life, there will be young boys and young girls playing in your home.*

And THE STREETS OF THE CITY SHALL BE FULL OF BOYS AND GIRLS PLAYING in the streets thereof.

Zechariah 8:5

4. **There will be marvelous blessings because of the presence of God.** Your life will be a life of wondrous and marvellous experiences because of the presence of God.

Thus saith the Lord of hosts; if IT BE MARVELLOUS in the eyes of the remnant of this people in these days, should it also be marvellous in mine eyes? saith the Lord of hosts.

Zechariah 8:6

5. **There will be great gatherings of God's people in churches and crusades and nations.** Because of the presence of God, there will be the salvation of many people. People will come from the east and the west. They will be gathered from all over. God will bring them and they will stay happily together in the house of the Lord in Jerusalem.

Thus saith the Lord of hosts; BEHOLD, I WILL SAVE my people from the east country, and from the west country; And I will bring them, and they shall dwell in the midst of

Jerusalem: and they shall be my people, and I will be their God, in truth and in righteousness.

Zechariah 8:7-8

6. **There will be strength to build God's house, physically and spiritually.** The presence of God will make our hands strong. Builders will arise and buildings will be built. Churches will be built because of the presence of God. We will no longer be in classrooms and tents because the presence of God will make our hands strong enough to build.

Thus saith the Lord of hosts; LET YOUR HANDS BE STRONG, ye that hear in these days these words by the mouth of the prophets, which were in the day that the foundation of the house of the Lord of hosts was laid, THAT THE TEMPLE MIGHT BE BUILT.

Zechariah 8:9

7. **There shall be jobs and prosperity because of the presence of God with the people.** Prosperity will come into the house because of the presence of God. Things will work as planned and the ground will give her increase. The heavens will give their dew because that is what is expected. God's people will possess all things because of the presence of God.

For before these days there was no hire for man, nor any hire for beast; neither was there any peace to him that went out or came in because of the affliction: for I set all men every one against his neighbour. But now I will not be unto the residue of this people as in the former days, saith the Lord of hosts.

FOR THE SEED SHALL BE PROSPEROUS; THE VINE SHALL GIVE HER FRUIT, AND THE GROUND SHALL GIVE HER INCREASE, AND THE HEAVENS SHALL GIVE THEIR DEW; AND I WILL CAUSE

THE REMNANT OF THIS PEOPLE TO POSSESS ALL THESE THINGS.

Zechariah 8:10-12

8. **There shall be a turnaround and you shall become a blessing to many instead of a source of concern and a curse.** You will be saved by the power of God.

And it shall come to pass, that as ye were a curse among the heathen, O house of Judah, and house of Israel; SO WILL I SAVE YOU, AND YE SHALL BE A BLESSING: fear not, but let your hands be strong.

Zechariah 8:13

9. **There shall be fastings, cheerful feasts and conventions.** Where the presence of God is, fasting will be a joy. Conventions and church activities will be a joy to those who love God's presence. Many people will love the truth of God's word because the presence of God is there.

Thus saith the Lord of hosts; THE FAST OF THE FOURTH MONTH, and the fast of the fifth, and the fast of the seventh, and the fast of the tenth, shall be to the house of Judah joy and gladness, and CHEERFUL FEASTS; therefore love the truth and peace.

Zechariah 8:19

10. **There shall come many people from afar.** Many people will come from many cities. Nowhere will be too far for people to come from. Your churches will be full of city dwellers who have come from afar.

Thus saith the Lord of hosts; It shall yet come to pass, that THERE SHALL COME PEOPLE, AND THE INHABITANTS OF MANY CITIES:

Zechariah 8:20

11. There shall be many prayer meetings where the presence of the Lord is. Prayer is a joy when the presence of God is there. People will rush to prayer meetings and crowd into churches. Where there is no presence, there are no prayer meetings!

> Thus saith the Lord of hosts; It shall yet come to pass, that there shall come people, and the inhabitants of many cities: And the inhabitants of one city shall go to another, saying, LET US GO SPEEDILY TO PRAY BEFORE THE LORD, and to seek the Lord of hosts: I will go also. Yea, many people and strong nations shall come to seek the Lord of hosts in Jerusalem, and to pray before the Lord.
>
> Zechariah 8:20-22

12. People will want to be with you because they recognize that God is with you. People will choose you! People will like you! People will opt to be with you! They will say, "I just want to be with you." They will say, "I just want to be in your company. I just want to go to your church. I just want to stay in your church."

> Yea, many people and strong nations shall come to seek the Lord of hosts in Jerusalem, and to pray before the Lord. Thus saith the Lord of hosts; In those days it shall come to pass, that ten men shall take hold out of all languages of the nations, even shall take hold of the skirt of him that is a Jew, saying, WE WILL GO WITH YOU: FOR WE HAVE HEARD THAT GOD IS WITH YOU.
>
> Zechariah 8:22-23

REFERENCES

Chapter 1

Excerpt taken from

Causes of Desolation. Retrieved from https://static1.squarespace.com/static/569e504b40667ab163697b9b/t/5b574df170a6ad46dfab346e/1532448241506/Rule_9.pdf - 10 April 2019

Made in the USA
Columbia, SC
08 January 2020